BIANCO

PIZZA, PASTA, AND OTHER FOOD I LIKE

CHRIS BIANCO

AN IMPRINT OF HARPERCOLLINSPUBLISHERS

BIANCO. Copyright © 2016 by Bianco Verde LLC. All rights reserved. Printed in the United States of America. No part of this book may be used or reproduced in any manner whatsoever without written permission except in the case of brief quotations embodied in critical articles and reviews. For information address HarperCollins Publishers, 195 Broadway, New York, NY 10007.

HarperCollins books may be purchased for educational, business, or sales promotional use. For information please e-mail the Special Markets Department at SPsales@harpercollins.com.

FIRST EDITION

Designed by Suet Yee Chong
Photographs by David Loftus

Library of Congress Cataloging-in-Publication Data has been applied for.

ISBN 978-0-06-222437-8 (hardcover)
ISBN 978-0-06-279105-4 (Williams Sonoma signed edition)

17 18 19 20 ID/QDG 10 9 8 7 6 5 4 3 2

TO MY FAMILY, PAST, PRESENT, AND FUTURE;
TO MY FRIENDS, BETTER KNOWN AS THE ONES WE CHOOSE;
AND TO GOD—ALL YOUR LOVE AND SUPPORT HAS BEEN,
AND IS, THE DRIVING FORCE OF MY EVERYTHING

CONTENTS

INTRODUCTION

The only thing stranger than me writing a book is the idea that anyone would read it. Whether you bought this, stole it, or received it as a gift that you plan to regift, thank you.

If you told me back in 1988, when I first opened Pizzeria Bianco in the back of a Phoenix supermarket, that anyone would ever give a shit about anything I had to say, I would have said, "Sure! And maybe I'll have a two-way wrist radio like Dick Tracy too! Get the fuck outta here."

But here I am, almost thirty years later, with a head of hair that is more salt than pepper, almost a real grown-up, married to my best friend, with two beautiful kids and friends and family who I love beyond my ability to articulate. These are my riches, and any successes I may have outside of these pale by comparison.

Love brought me to the table and helped me stumble through the kitchen. I watched as my mom, aunts, and grandmothers made something delicious, and I watched how people responded to it. How I responded to it. It was an expression of love and, though I didn't know it then, I wanted to be a part of it.

Knowing where our food comes from is as important as knowing where we come from. What we eat has history, purpose, and value. The choices we make affect our bodies and our planet. None of this was on my radar when I was a kid ironing a foil-wrapped grilled cheese sandwich after school, but now it colors everything I do. We need only submit to nature's perfection and from there imagine the possibilities. An heirloom apple hanging heavy on a crisp autumn day might need only a rub on your shirtsleeve to illuminate its perfection.

My hope is that this book can help you to appreciate how much you already know. A delicious pizza is no more mysterious or magical than the omelettes you make on Sundays or the grilled cheese sandwich you've been perfecting for twenty years. The same principles apply. Use the best ingredients you can and keep at it. Don't quit. You learn things when you burn things.

When it's perfect or close to it, recognize why, remember what you did, and repeat again and again until your children ask you to teach them to make it.

This is not the last book or the "final word" on pizza, pasta, or anything else, but I hope you will find something in it of worth.

Love,
Chris

**My brother, Marco; my grandfather
Leonard "Big Sonny" Bianco; and me.**

PIZZA

LOVE & MASTERS

Understanding and appropriating these two words has been a ghost in my machine for as long as I can remember. Take the word "master": as far as I'm concerned we could do ourselves much good by just removing it from our vocabulary. The terms "pizza master," "bread master," or "whatever master" create a submissive or unequal relationship when they're applied to food and all that makes coming to the table possible. When I am kneading or shaping dough, I rely solely on being present and responding to how much something needs, whether it's just time or manipulation—I knead you and I need you. If someone asked me what business I was in, I'd say the

relationship business—understanding the importance of relationships and my role in them applies to food, people, furniture, you name it. I want us both to be happy.

As for love, that's a bit broader. I see love only as a four-letter word that does its best to explain what in most cases is unexplainable—we love our dogs, cats, friends, wives, husbands, family, God, and, yes, pizza. It's taken my whole life thus far to get them in order and serve them appropriately. If I do all my most diligent foraging and preparation but am negligent on oven temperature or vessel or lack of a plate to put the food on, my intention will be at risk. Back in the late '80s when wood ovens weren't so popular, some people would watch me work and say, "The wood-fired oven—*that's* the secret." The secret that is no secret is even in the most Ferrari of ovens, shit in will be shit out, yet the most humble oven at the proper temperature with all aspects in balance and restrained harmony, will set you free.

PIZZA DOUGH

This dough contains just four ingredients: water, flour, yeast, and salt. Let's consider each one in turn. Before you make the dough for the first time, I want you to pour yourself a glass of the water you'll be using and drink it. I want you to really taste it. It is going to rehydrate the flour, and its warmth will bring the yeast back to life. Ask yourself how salty it is, how sweet it is. Record your observations.

Next, think about the flour. What kind are you going to use? I like one that is high in protein (13 to 14 pcl, organic, and grown and freshly milled as close to home as possible), because it gives the finished crust a good chew. If you're lucky enough to have a mill near where you live, pay a visit and ask about its flour and grain varietal. The flour is the biggest single factor in the flavor of your dough, so it's something that you don't want to compromise on.

Now the yeast. Yeast is life. Yeast is what makes bread different from everything else we eat. Here, for ease, I use active dry yeast. As you experiment, you may want to try fresh yeast, but active dry yeast will give you a good and consistent result.

And last, salt. Salt is flavor. It's rare to see someone muck up a bread with too much salt. If anything, I find a lot of bread is insipid because it lacks salt. Pick a fine, not coarse, salt you like, preferably sea salt that has been minimally processed.

Makes enough for four 10-inch pizzas

1 envelope (2¼ teaspoons; 9 grams) active dry yeast
2 cups warm water (105° to 110°F)
5 to 5½ cups bread or other high-protein flour, preferably organic and freshly milled, plus more for dusting

2 teaspoons (12 grams) fine sea salt
Extra virgin olive oil, for greasing the bowl

Combine the yeast and warm water in a large bowl. Give the yeast a stir to help dissolve it, and let it do its thing for 5 minutes. You're giving it a little bit of a kick-start, giving it some room to activate, to breathe.

When the yeast has dissolved, stir in 3 cups of the flour, mixing gently until smooth. You're letting the flour marry the yeast. Slowly add 2 cups more flour, working it in gently. You should be able to smell the yeast working—that happy yeasty smell. Add the salt. (If you add the salt earlier, it could inhibit the yeast's growth.) If necessary, add up to ½ cup more flour 1 tablespoon at a time, stirring until the dough comes away from the bowl but is still sticky.

Turn the dough out onto a floured work surface and get to work. Slap the dough onto the counter, pulling it toward you with one hand while pushing it away with the other, stretching it and folding it back on itself. Repeat the process until the dough is noticeably easier to handle, 10 to 15 times, then knead until it's smooth and stretchy, soft, and still a little tacky. This should take about 10 minutes, but here, feel is everything. (One of the most invaluable tools I have in my kitchen is a plastic dough scraper. It costs next to nothing, and it allows me to make sure that no piece of dough is left behind.)

Shape the dough into a ball and put it in a lightly greased big bowl. Roll the dough around to coat it with oil, then cover the bowl with plastic wrap and let the dough rest in a warm place until it doubles in size, 3 to 5 hours. When you press the fully proofed dough with your finger, the indentation should remain.

Turn the proofed dough out onto a floured work surface and cut it into 4 pieces. Roll the pieces into balls and dust them with flour. Cover with plastic wrap and let them rest for another hour, or until they have doubled in size.

The dough is ready to be shaped, topped, and baked. If you don't want to make 4 pizzas at a time, the dough balls can be wrapped well and refrigerated for up 8 hours or frozen for up to 3 weeks; thaw in the refrigerator and let come to room temperature before proceeding.

SHAPING PIZZA DOUGH

Hold the top edge of a piece of dough with both hands, allowing the bottom edge to touch the work surface, and carefully move your hands around the edges to form a circle of dough. You have to find your own style, but I usually just cup my hand into a C shape, turn my hand knuckle side up, and drape the dough off it, allowing gravity to do its work, so it gently falls onto the floured table. Imagine you're turning a wheel. Hold that dough aloft, allowing its weight to stretch it into a rough 10-inch circle. Don't put any pressure on it by pulling or stretching it, just let gravity do the job—

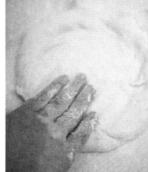

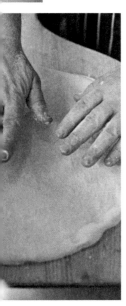

you want that aeration and cragginess. Keep it moving, and it will start to relax—like we relax when we are on a sofa.

At this point, you're ready to make a pizza. Lay the dough on a lightly floured pizza peel or inverted baking sheet. Gently press out the edges with your fingers. You will start to see some puffiness or bubbles now. Jerk the peel to make sure the dough is not sticking. If it is, lift the dough and dust the underside with a little flour (or, if no one is looking, blow under it very gently). Tuck and shape it until it's a happy circle.

Top the pizza as per the instructions in any of the recipes that follow.

PROOFING DOUGH

In our Pizza Dough recipe, you proof the dough for up to 2½ hours, then divide it into balls and let it proof for another hour before you bake it. It tastes good. No problems. But what happens if you proof it for 7 hours? What if you let it go for 24 hours? Or 36? Or 48? It will be different, and that difference might be more to your taste than the basic dough. At 3 to 5 hours for the first proof, you will have a dough that will brown more quickly than a dough that's proofed for 14 hours, because the yeast will not have converted as many of the sugars. The longer the dough proofs, and the more sugars are converted, the more it will have that smell of fermentation, and the more the sour flavors will develop. Many people (including me) love those flavors—like in a good sourdough bread—but here I don't necessarily want too many of them, because I don't want them to dominate the flavors of the pizza toppings. That said, there is no wrong way to go here. Make the dough a few times, following the recipe, until you feel comfortable. Then start to play with it. Determine how long a proof you like.

Bear in mind that where you are in the world will also play its part. If you're making the dough in Iceland, it's going to be different from making it in Phoenix. The climate is different, so it may need to proof for a little longer than 3 to 5 hours to start. Your water will be different, and it will affect the flavor of your dough. Never forget, we're dealing with only four ingredients, and each one brings its own flavors and qualities to the pizza. So record the process as you go. Work with your sense of taste and your broader sensibility of the things you like. This basic dough recipe is only an early survey of a journey you get to finish yourself. The possibilities are endless.

CRUSHED TOMATO SAUCE

This is the sauce we use the most at our restaurants. It couldn't be simpler. People are often surprised when they find out the sauce is uncooked, but canning tomatoes partially cooks them, and the heat of the oven finishes the process. The next question we usually get is why we don't use fresh tomatoes, especially when our restaurants focus on seasonal ingredients. But fresh tomatoes are not always the best choice for sauce. The window for perfect ripe tomatoes isn't very long, and in winter, pallid grocery store tomatoes are going to give you a real bummer of a sauce. One of the many beauties of pizza is that it relies on ingredients you can always have on hand. You just need a well-stocked pantry.

Beautifully canned or jarred tomatoes, preferably organic and delicious, are a celebration of height-of-season produce, a moment captured in time and available to you long after summer has gone. My partner, Rob DiNapoli, and I have our own Bianco DiNapoli brand canned tomatoes that we use at our restaurants. The tomatoes are organic and harvested in peak season and packed within hours. They're steam-peeled and then canned in tomato juice (about 3 ounces of juice per 28-ounce can).

We don't add any stabilizers, but we do add a bit of sea salt, because we found that adding a pinch of salt at canning resulted in more depth of flavor. So, because our canned tomatoes contain a scant amount of salt, we don't add salt when making this sauce. Be alert to the salt content of whatever canned tomatoes you use. Don't just read the label—taste them before using them. Cooking will reduce the sauce and the saltiness will become more pronounced, so you want to be on the lighter side of salinity when you set out—on the road to perfection instead of already at the destination.

We also include four fresh basil leaves in every can. When you macerate the tomatoes as you make the sauce, you'll infuse them with the basil. Not all canned tomatoes include basil. This recipe calls for adding fresh basil to the sauce. If your tomatoes already include the herb, taste them and see if you want to take it a step further or if you're happy with them as is. We always add a few hand-bruised fresh leaves too.

Makes enough for four 10-inch pizzas

One 28-ounce can whole tomatoes
1 generous tablespoon extra virgin
   olive oil
4 or 5 fresh basil leaves, torn and
   bruised (optional if the canned
   tomatoes include basil; see
   headnote)

Fine sea salt (optional)

Empty the can of tomatoes, with their juice, into a large bowl. Add the olive oil with the basil and salt (if using) and using your hands, crush the tomatoes; discard any bits of skin or hard yellow "shoulders," or cores. The better the tomato, the less likely you are to find shoulders and hard cores. You want to end up with a textured yet silky sauce. I like it when the sauce isn't uniform, when there are still bits and pieces of tomato; I also don't like using an immersion blender or food processor because these can bring out the bitterness of the seeds. A hand-crushed sauce has a better mouthfeel and won't be so one-dimensional.

     Time is the invisible ingredient here, so if you can, let the sauce sit for about an hour so the flavors can marry. Of course, in our restaurants, we don't always have the luxury of that time, and the sauce is still great.

PIZZA MARGHERITA

Almost everyone knows a Margherita pizza, or at least a cheese pizza. For me, that widespread familiarity was an opportunity to exceed people's expectations, to check off the requisite boxes but go above and beyond with optimal ingredients. The Margherita is the quintessential Neapolitan pizza—hell, let's just say it is *the* quintessential pizza. Its much-debated origin is as much a tale of national identity as it is of pizza. The story goes that back in 1889, just twenty-eight years after Italy had been unified as a country, Queen Margherita of Savoy and her king, Umberto I, were touring the nation to encourage a sense of nationalism. In the south especially, people were still angry about the loss of their independence; they weren't easy days. So it seems especially powerful that it was in Naples, stronghold of southern Italy, that the most emblematic style of the arguably most emblematic dish of Italy was born. Legend has it that Margherita had noticed people across the country eating pizza, and she wanted to try it. Whether she was just curious or was trying to align herself with the common people, we can't know, but I love the idea of a queen drawing closer to her subjects through food. Neapolitan chef Raffaele Esposito presented her with a tomato, mozzarella, and basil pizza—the red, white, and green mirroring the colors of the new Italian flag—and named the pizza in her honor. To me, the beauty of this story is that it embodies my motivating belief that food is about so much more than physical sustenance or pleasure. It's about identity and place and relationships—and how the best food happens when we begin with an intention and work from a place of attention, just as Raffaele did for his queen.

Note: This recipe is more detailed than the pizza recipes that follow—you can think of it as a master recipe for assembling and baking pizza.

The Margherita is perfect as is, but it's also a perfect canvas for other ingredients. Just remember that when you add or remove something from a pizza, you need to accommodate for that gain or loss, be it a matter of texture, moisture, flavor, or the like. For example, adding ricotta cheese could make your pizza more watery, so you'd want to use a little less tomato sauce to balance things out.

Makes one 10-inch pizza

One ball Pizza Dough (page 4), rested
and ready to shape

2 ounces fresh mozzarella, torn into
cubes

6 tablespoons Crushed Tomato Sauce
(page 8), with an added glug of extra
virgin olive oil

A pinch or two of finely grated
Parmigiano-Reggiano (optional)

Fine sea salt (optional)

Extra virgin olive oil, for drizzling

5 fresh basil leaves

Position a rack in the lower third of the oven (remove the rack above it) and place a pizza stone on it. Turn up your oven to its maximum setting, as high as it will go, and let that baby preheat for a solid hour. Don't even bother putting together your pizza until the oven's been going for an hour.

Once the oven is preheated, grab a pizza peel and give it a nice, light dusting of flour. This will help prevent the pizza from sticking when you slide it from peel to stone. (If you don't have a peel, you can use a cookie sheet or an inverted baking sheet.)

Shape the dough as directed on page 5 and set the prepared dough on the peel. Jerk the peel to make sure it's not sticking. If it is, lift the dough and dust the underside with extra flour (or, if no one is looking, blow under it very gently). Tuck and shape it until it's a happy circle.

Taste your mozzarella and your tomato sauce to see how salty they both are and make a mental note of this. Spoon the tomato sauce evenly over the pizza, using the back of the spoon to spread the sauce, starting from the center and stopping about ¾ inch—a fat thumb's width—from the edges. (With a hand-crushed tomato sauce, the consistency of the sauce over the pizza's surface will be uneven. It's inevitable.) Sprinkle the Parmigiano, if using, over the sauce. Let the spots where the tomato sauce is thinner guide you as to the placement of the mozzarella—hit those drier spots with a bit more mozzarella. If when you tasted your sauce and cheese earlier you determined that the salinity wasn't quite there yet, sprinkle the pizza with some salt. Then give it a very light drizzle of olive oil.

Open the oven and, tilting the peel just slightly, give it a quick shimmy-shake to slide the pizza onto the pizza stone. Bake the pizza for 10 to 15 minutes, until the crust is crisp and golden brown.

Remove the pizza with the peel and immediately add the basil leaves, laying them evenly across the top. The heat of the pizza will wilt the leaves slightly and release their heady fragrance. Enjoy immediately!

BEFORE OR AFTER

Most traditional recipes call for basil to be cooked with the pizza, which is totally fine. I prefer tearing and rough-handling fresh basil leaves over the cooked pizza and letting the heat release the aroma. The essential oils from the basil provide a pleasing texture and flavor profile.

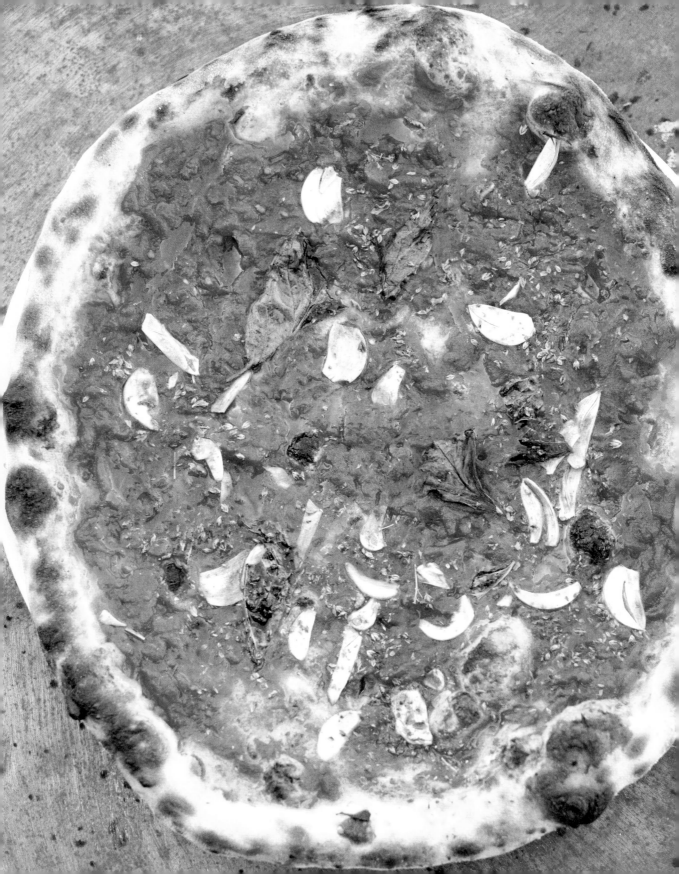

PIZZA MARINARA

For me, the marinara is the most difficult pizza to make, but it is also without a doubt my favorite one. Its minimalism at first glance could easily belie its complexity. The difficulty lies in two factors: The first is a matter of chemistry. Unlike the Margherita, the marinara does not have the luxury of cheese; it's just sauce, herbs, and garlic, twice as much sauce, in fact, as the Margherita. So it's saucier than your usual pie, and there is a little bit of a dance involved. You want to hit that sweet spot with the cooking time where the pizza is still moist with sauce but not soggy. The second bit of difficulty also goes back to that no-cheese thing. In a marinara, there are no distractions—there is nowhere to hide. It is a study in minimalism.

And that's why it is so near and dear to my heart. It is a pizza of ultimate nakedness, transparency, humility, and grace, made with the most humble of ingredients. It is about transforming a few pantry staples into a sublime whole so much greater than the sum of its parts, through an act of sustained focus and appreciation for the task at hand. If I had the pleasure of cooking for you and you said, "Chris, make *anything*!" this would be my go-to.

Makes one 10-inch pizza

One ball Pizza Dough (page 4), rested and ready to shape
¾ cup Crushed Tomato Sauce (page 8)
A pinch of dried oregano, preferably wild

2 garlic cloves, sliced paper-thin
1 or 2 fresh basil leaves
Extra virgin olive oil, for drizzling
Coarse sea salt
Crushed red pepper flakes (optional)

Position a rack in the lower third of the oven (remove the rack above it) and place a pizza stone on it. Turn up your oven to its maximum setting and let that baby preheat for a solid hour.

Once the oven is preheated, grab a pizza peel and give it a nice, light dusting of flour. Shape the dough as directed on page 5 and set the prepared dough on the peel. Jerk the peel to make sure it's not sticking. If it is, lift the dough and dust the underside with extra flour (or, if no one is looking, blow under it very gently). Tuck and shape it until it's a happy circle.

Spoon the tomato sauce evenly over the pizza, using the back of the spoon to spread the sauce, starting from the center and stopping about ¾ inch—a fat thumb's width—from the edges. (With a hand-crushed tomato sauce, the consistency of the sauce over the pizza's surface will be uneven. It's inevitable.) Add the oregano, pinching it firmly as you sprinkle it over the sauce to activate its aroma. Scatter the sliced garlic evenly over the top. Finally, bruise the basil leaves, tear them (for little nuggets of brightness), and place them in the center of the pizza. Drizzle on a little extra virgin olive oil.

Open the oven and, tilting the peel just slightly, give it a quick shimmy-shake to slide the pizza onto the pizza stone. Bake the pizza for 10 to 15 minutes, until the crust is crisp and golden brown. This is a fairly wet pizza, so it may take a little longer than others.

Remove the pizza with the peel, drizzle on a little olive oil, and finish with a sprinkle of coarse sea salt. You could even dust it with a crumble of red pepper flakes for a slight quickening of its cadence in your mouth. Enjoy immediately!

WILD OREGANO

We use dried local wild oregano in a range of dishes. It's dried on the stem, and we just crumble the leaves into the pot (or over a pizza), releasing all the intense fragrance and the flavorful oil. Dried wild oregano on the stem from Greece and other areas of the Mediterranean is available from some gourmet markets and online spice purveyors. If you can't get it, use good-quality dried oregano, but be sure to crush the leaves between your fingertips as you add them to whatever you are cooking.

PIZZA BIANCOVERDE

At the pizzeria, when I sat down to write out the final menu, I wanted there to be a balance of three pies with tomato sauce and three without. At the time, white pies weren't really common in the States, at least outside the East Coast, where white pizza—typically a rubbery stretch of overcooked mozzarella pocked with scoops of deli ricotta—was a standard in most slice joints. But I had had beautiful white pies in Rome, and had a lasting memory of a particularly killer *quattro formaggi*—the classic four-cheese pizza— that was rich but not heavy. So at first I thought I'd do a quattro formaggi too. But after thinking about my setup—How much room did I have on my line? How many of the cheeses could I reach quickly as I cooked? And how many great, high-quality Italian cheeses were readily available in Phoenix back then?—I settled on a three-cheese pizza with mozzarella, Parmigiano-Reggiano, and fresh ricotta. Three Italian classics, but familiar to Americans. Three significant textures that work well together and taste delicious: the pliant quality of the mozzarella, the fatty sharpness of the Parmigiano, and the yielding creaminess of ricotta. Then I'd offset the buttery dairy goodness of the cheeses with barely wilted peppery arugula—a bright hit of something green and fresh.

With this pizza—with all white pies, really—the cut of the cheese is of paramount importance, because how you break down your cheese will determine its texture once it is cooked. This pie is all about the subtle textural differences among the cheeses, which underscore the differences in their flavors. You want to tear the mozzarella into cubes that will melt into shreds of cheese that have some chew. For the Parmesan, use the large holes on a box grater; if the cheese is finely grated, it will break down too quickly and toughen. For the ricotta, you don't need to break it down, of course, but you do want to think about the size of the spoon you use to dollop it on the pizza. I like to use a teaspoon so there are substantial but not overwhelming moments of creaminess.

For the Biancoverde, I like a younger Parmigiano, in the 24-to-36-month range. A Parmigiano aged for 2 years has a great maturity and all that awesome developed flavor, but it also still has good moisture content. I love older Parms—don't get me wrong—but I think they're better for straight-up eating rather than cooking.

Makes one 10-inch pizza

One ball Pizza Dough (page 4), rested and ready to shape

1 ounce Parmigiano-Reggiano, coarsely grated

1 ounce fresh mozzarella, torn into cubes

2 tablespoons whole-milk ricotta, drained of whey

A good handful of wild or baby arugula

Extra virgin olive oil, for drizzling

Coarse sea salt and freshly ground black pepper

Position a rack in the lower third of the oven (remove the rack above it) and place a pizza stone on it. Turn up your oven to its maximum setting and let that baby preheat for a solid hour.

Once the oven is preheated, grab a pizza peel and give it a nice, light dusting of flour. Shape the dough as directed on page 5 and set the dough on the floured peel. Jerk the peel to make sure it's not sticking. If it is, lift the dough and dust the underside with extra flour (or, if no one is looking, blow under it very gently). Tuck and shape it until it's a happy circle.

Scatter the Parmigiano evenly over the surface of the dough, stopping about ¾ inch—a fat thumb's width—from the edges. Scatter the mozzarella over the Parmigiano. Finally, gently spoon on the ricotta in small dollops, aiming for a nice even balance.

Open the oven and, tilting the peel just slightly, give it a quick shimmy-shake to slide the pizza onto the pizza stone. Bake the pizza for 10 to 15 minutes, until the crust is crisp and golden brown. White pizzas like this have a tendency to set more quickly, so this may take slightly less time in the oven than most pizzas.

Remove the pizza with the peel and immediately scatter the arugula evenly over the top. The heat of the pizza will wilt the greens just enough to make them tender, but they will still hold their shape. Finish the pizza with a drizzle of beautiful olive oil and a few pinches of coarse salt and turns of black pepper. Enjoy immediately!

PIZZA ROSA

Over the years, a number of people have asked me how I invented this pizza. The thing is, to my mind, a chef laying claim to invention is a rejection of inspiration, of influence, of history. The Rosa is entirely me paying homage to an inspiration. Almost thirty years ago, I spent an afternoon in Finale Ligure, an old port town in Liguria. I had lunch at a little *focacceria*. For Ligurians, focaccia—specifically *focaccia Genovese*—is what pizza is to Neapolitans, and Liguria is known throughout Italy as the home of the best focaccia in the country. The focacceria in question was next door to a *salumeria,* and it turned out that a father-son duo ran the two shops. The menu at the focacceria was short and sweet. I ordered a simple but unusual Parmesan and sesame seed focaccia. The son brought it out on a small plate, on which were nestled a few delicate shavings of cured meat from the salumeria. As I ate, I would drape a bit of meat on a bite of the bread and follow that with a cold sip of a white wine from Veneto. The whole thing was transcendent. It was way better than it had any right to be.

As soon as I got home, I tried replicating it. No dice. First of all, my pop didn't run a salumeria next door to me. I attempted to get it right a few more times, but the results were always disappointing; nothing I made could match the impact of that Finale Ligure focaccia. I knew part of it had to be the sesame seeds. The town had a long history as a stop for ships bearing goods from Asia and Africa, and its cuisine reflects that influence. And there, the sesame seeds, delicate and volatile, hadn't had to travel for nearly as far as they would to reach me in Arizona. So I started thinking less about how to copy the focaccia and more about how to evoke its spirit. What was it that had spoken to me so urgently? Well, I loved how it did so much with so little. I loved its connection to place, how something as small as a sesame seed symbolized the town's unique history and culture. I loved the play and echo of the nutty seeds against the Parmesan, which already has that quality of nuttiness.

I started thinking about what we had of worth in Arizona, of the singular ingredient, like the sesame seeds, that would remind people that what they were eating was *from* somewhere. What I came up with was our pistachios, grown here and plentiful in southern Arizona, fresh, bright, and beautiful married with some Parmigiano-Reggiano. But the pistachios and Parmesan needed something else, something with a spice to it. We had tons of rosemary growing around our building, and the woody herbaceous quality of the bruised leaves went perfectly with the nuts and cheese. I was getting close, but I found I wanted another texture. There was something about that original, by now mythic, focaccia that had reminded me of the bialys of my childhood. And the best part of those bialys was the melted, chewy onions that tended to collect at their centers. So I added red onions, sliced thin and tossed in olive oil until they wilted, and the Rosa was born: I named the pizza after the pink of the red onion.

This is a pizza of restraint that delivers tenfold on its first bite.

Makes one 10-inch pizza

One ball Pizza Dough (page 4), rested and ready to shape
3 ounces Parmigiano-Reggiano, coarsely grated
Scant ¼ cup paper-thin slices red onion

Leaves from ½ rosemary sprig
A small handful of unsalted roasted pistachios, crushed
Extra virgin olive oil, for drizzling

Position a rack in the lower third of the oven (remove the rack above it) and place a pizza stone on it. Turn up your oven to its maximum setting and let that baby preheat for a solid hour.

Once the oven is preheated, grab a pizza peel and give it a nice, light dusting of flour. Shape the dough as directed on page 5 and set the dough on the floured peel. Jerk the peel to make sure it's not sticking. If it is, lift the dough and dust the underside with extra flour (or, if no one is looking, blow under it very gently). Tuck and shape it until it's a happy circle.

Scatter the Parmigiano evenly over the pizza, stopping about ¾ inch—a fat thumb's width—from the edges. Scatter the onions and then the rosemary—pinching it to lightly bruise it and release its oils as you go—evenly over the top.

Open the oven and, tilting the peel just slightly, give it a quick shimmy-shake to slide the pizza onto the pizza stone. After about 5 minutes, quickly scatter the pistachios over the pizza. Bake the pizza for 5 to 10 minutes longer, until the crust is crisp and golden brown.

Remove the pizza with the peel and drizzle with a good glug of olive oil. Enjoy immediately!

SONNY BOY PIZZA

This pizza was born of two contradictory impulses. On the one hand, I wanted to do a pizza that I felt like someone from the old neighborhood would dig, something they would recognize. To me, pepperoni pizza is an iconic New York–style pizza. On the other hand, I wanted to somehow preempt people's tendency to order automatically, like "Give me a cheese pepperoni!" and so I could say to customers, "Well, we don't have *that*, but you might like *this*." I sought out a really good-quality soppressata, which has a similar fattiness and spice profile to pepperoni. I love the coarse texture of it, all that good porkiness and salinity, which is so beautiful married with the acidity of the tomato sauce. But you could also use finocchiona, coppa, or your favorite salami—or, if you like, by all means pepperoni.

I don't usually use a lot of olives, but I like them here, both because they echo the canned black olives that might share space with old-school pepperoni pies and because the combination of olives and salami reminds me of a classic antipasti plate. And for me, the Sonny Boy is kind of like an antipasto. It's my favorite of the pizzas to share and to have a slice or two. And it's almost too salty, in a good way, without going over that edge. In case you're wondering, I named it after my dad. Sonny Boy was his nickname growing up—he hated it, and I'm a smart-ass. He likes the pizza, though.

Getting the salt balance right is the make-or-break factor for this pie, and you have the best opportunity to refine that by tweaking the olives you use. Make sure you taste them, before you add them to the pie. If they're super salty, you'll want to cut back on them. You're looking for balance with the fat, acidity, and crispy bits.

Makes one 10-inch pizza

One ball Pizza Dough (page 4), rested and ready to shape
6 tablespoons Crushed Tomato Sauce (page 8)

A pinch or two of finely grated Parmigiano-Reggiano (optional)
2 ounces fresh mozzarella, torn into cubes

(ingredients continue on next page)

1½ ounces thinly sliced soppressata
(about 10 slices)
8 to 10 Kalamata, Gaeta, or your
favorite olives, split and pitted

A pinch of dried oregano, preferably
wild

Position a rack in the lower third of the oven (remove the rack above it) and place a pizza stone on it. Turn up your oven to its maximum setting and let that baby preheat for a solid hour.

Grab a pizza peel and give it a nice, light dusting of flour. Shape the dough as directed on page 5 and set the dough on the floured peel. Jerk the peel to make sure it's not sticking. If it is, lift the dough and dust the underside with extra flour (or, if no one is looking, blow under it very gently). Tuck and shape it until it's a happy circle.

Spoon the tomato sauce evenly over the pizza, using the back of the spoon to help spread it, starting from the center and stopping about ¾ inch—a fat thumb's width—from the edges. (With a hand-crushed tomato sauce, the consistency of the sauce over the pizza's surface will be uneven. It's inevitable.) Sprinkle the Parmigiano, if using, over the sauce. Let the spots where the tomato sauce is thinner guide you as to the placement of the mozzarella—hit those drier spots with a bit more mozzarella. Add the soppressata, spacing it evenly, followed by the olives. Then crumble the oregano over the pizza, pinching it firmly to activate its flavor and aroma.

Open the oven and, tilting the peel just slightly, give it a quick shimmy-shake to slide the pizza onto the pizza stone. Bake the pizza for 10 to 15 minutes, until the crust is crisp and golden brown.

Remove the pizza with the peel. Enjoy immediately!

WISEGUY PIZZA

Yes, sometimes less is still too much. But other times, well . . . sometimes more is still not enough, and that's the spirit of the Wiseguy. The Wiseguy is a bit over the top on purpose and tips the scales of balance to the max. It's got a sense of humor. At the time this pizza came into being, the movie *Goodfellas* was immensely popular, and I found myself thinking, *What would I make if a guy like Paulie rolled up to my shop?* I'd want it to be pretty special but not take itself too seriously. So here we are: smoked mozzarella, onions roasted in our wood-burning oven, and fennel sausage. A reimagined sausage pizza. The mozzarella is almost nutty from the pecan wood we use to smoke it, the onions are a little leathery and toothsome, and the sausage tastes almost piney. Each ingredient brings a specific flavor profile that balances the others: You've got elements of sweet, salty, fatty, campfire, woodsiness. And each ingredient has its own distinct texture. I wanted a pie I could pick at, and pull things off of with my fingers: I love the snap of a good sausage, and here we cut the sausage on the diagonal so it will curl slightly as it cooks and so you can see the interior. The roasted onions, redolent of char from that hot oven, are in thick slices, so you have to bite into them. The mozzarella has the chew you expect but surprises with its smokiness. I've always loved smoked mozzarella—when I was a kid, it was probably the most exotic thing I ate. If you can't find it, substitute smoked Gouda or a smoked young cheddar. At our restaurants, we do a really quick hot smoke on the cheese because I don't want it to be too acrid, or it would overpower the pizza. Of course, you could just use fresh mozzarella, if smoke is not your thing.

If you want a great little antipasto, cook some onions as in this recipe, then dress them with balsamic vinegar, some toasted or fried coarse bread crumbs, and a little grated pecorino.

Makes one 10-inch pizza

1 large white or yellow onion, sliced into thick rings

1 tablespoon extra virgin olive oil, plus more for drizzling

Fine sea salt and freshly ground black pepper

¼ cup loosely packed fresh flat-leaf parsley leaves

(ingredients continue on next page)

One ball Pizza Dough (page 4), rested and ready to shape
2 ounces smoked mozzarella, smoked Gouda, or smoked cheddar, sliced or cut into cubes
½ pound sweet Italian sausages, or your favorite sausages, cooked (grilled, panfried, or roasted, as you like) and thinly sliced on the diagonal
Coarse sea salt

Position a rack in the lower third of the oven (remove the rack above it) and preheat the oven to 400°F.

Arrange the onion slices on a rimmed baking sheet and drizzle with the 1 tablespoon olive oil, then carefully turn them so they're evenly coated with oil. Season with fine sea salt and pepper and pop them into the oven for 10 minutes. Carefully turn the onion slices and cook for 10 more minutes. Toss them well and cook for about 10 minutes longer; you want them to get a beautiful color, a good golden brown, and to cook down significantly but still have integrity. Scrape them into a bowl and toss them with the parsley. Set aside.

Place a pizza stone on the oven rack and increase the oven temperature to its maximum setting. Since the oven is already hot, another 20 minutes or so of preheating should do it.

Grab a pizza peel and give it a nice, light dusting of flour. Shape the dough as directed on page 5 and set the dough on the floured peel. Jerk the peel to make sure it's not sticking. If it is, lift the dough and dust the underside with extra flour (or, if no one is looking, blow under it very gently). Tuck and shape it until it's a happy circle.

Hit the dough with the mozzarella, scattering it evenly and stopping about ¾ inch—a fat thumb's width—from the edges. Add the caramelized onion slices, draping them over the spots where there's less cheese. Finally, add the sausage, arranging it to balance the cheese and onion.

Open the oven and, tilting the peel just slightly, give it a quick shimmy-shake to slide the pizza onto the pizza stone. Bake the pizza for 10 to 15 minutes, until the crust is crisp and golden brown.

Remove the pizza with the peel, sprinkle with a pinch of coarse salt, and drizzle with olive oil. Enjoy immediately!

FOCACCIA

You could also call this Sicilian pizza or *pizza al taglio* or grandma pie—it can be any of those. Even the name "grandma pie" makes me happy, because it makes me think of a grandma in Topeka or Chicago, someone who doesn't have a wood-burning oven and makes pizza in a pan because she's busy. But here I wanted to evoke a version of the Sicilian pizza I loved growing up in New York. Sicilian pie wasn't an everyday thing. It was bigger than life. It was rare to see it available as slices. I loved the crust, the crispy oiliness of it, the crunchy bottom that gave way to an airy, springy center and a tender, yielding top. Sicilian pizza always felt celebratory.

This is the same dough we use to make pizza, but it is given a slightly longer proofing time after the first rise. We also use this focaccia, without any topping other than coarse salt and maybe some rosemary leaves, for our sandwiches.

Makes 9 large pieces for sandwiches or 12 smaller pieces

Pizza Dough (page 4), taken through the 3-hour rise
¼ cup extra virgin olive oil
Coarse sea salt (optional)

Chopped fresh rosemary or another topping of your choice (optional; recipes follow)

After the dough has proofed for a minimum of 3 hours, put it on a large rimmed baking sheet and drizzle the oil over it, turning to coat. Then flatten and press the dough out into a rectangle (it won't fill the pan entirely at this point). Cover with plastic wrap and let proof for 1½ hours in a warm place. When the dough has fully proofed, it will have absorbed some of the oil, will have stretched to fit the pan snugly, and will look alive, almost bubbling.

Meanwhile, about an hour before the dough has finished proofing, preheat the oven to its highest setting.

Using two fingers, make even indentations in rows up and down the surface of the dough, leaving a 1-inch border all around. At this point, you can just sprinkle it with some sea salt and, if you like, fresh rosemary leaves and bake it as directed (that is the version we use for our sandwiches) or you can use one of the toppings that follow. The choice is yours.

TOMATO, PARMESAN, AND HERB TOPPING

Makes enough for 1 focaccia

1 cup Crushed Tomato Sauce (page 8)
¾ pound Parmigiano-Reggiano,
   coarsely grated

A pinch of dried oregano, preferably
   wild, or a few fresh basil leaves
Extra virgin olive oil, for drizzling

Spoon the tomato sauce onto the dough, using the back of the spoon to spread it evenly and leaving a 1-inch border all around. Scatter the grated Parmigiano evenly over the tomato sauce and then sprinkle on the oregano, pinching it with your fingers to release all that heady scent. Finish with a few good lashes of olive oil.

   Transfer the pan to the oven and bake for 15 minutes. Rotate the pan front to back and bake for about 15 minutes more, until the focaccia is golden brown. Remove it from the pan, transfer to a wire rack, and cool for at least 10 minutes. Cut into squares and serve warm.

FIG, RED ONION, PECORINO, AND THYME TOPPING

Makes enough for 1 focaccia

1 cup fig jam
About 2 tablespoons water
2 red onions, thinly sliced into rings
¼ pound young pecorino or Manchego, shaved

Leaves from 3 thyme sprigs
Leaves from 1 or 2 rosemary sprigs
Sea salt and freshly ground black pepper
Extra virgin olive oil, for drizzling

Combine the jam with 2 tablespoons water in a small saucepan and warm over low heat, stirring, until the jam is the consistency of honey, adding a little more water if needed. Remove from the heat.

Spoon the jam over the dough, using the back of the spoon to spread it evenly and leaving a 1-inch border all around. Scatter the onions evenly over the jam, then follow with the pecorino. Sprinkle the herbs over the top. Season with salt and pepper and finish with a few good lashes of olive oil.

Transfer the pan to the oven and bake for 15 minutes. Rotate the pan front to back and bake for about 15 minutes more, until the focaccia is golden brown. Remove it from the pan, transfer to a wire rack, and cool for at least 10 minutes. Cut into squares and serve warm.

LEMON, PECORINO, AND RED ONION TOPPING

Makes enough for 1 focaccia

½ pound young pecorino or Manchego, thinly shaved

2 lemons, sliced into paper-thin rounds and seeds removed

½ red onion, very thinly sliced into rings

Leaves from 1 rosemary sprig

¼ teaspoon fine sea salt

Extra virgin olive oil, for drizzling

Scatter the pecorino over the dough, leaving a 1-inch border all around. Arrange the lemon slices evenly over the pecorino and follow with the onion slices. Sprinkle the rosemary over the top and season with the salt. Finish with a few good lashes of olive oil.

Transfer the pan to the oven and bake for 15 minutes. Rotate the pan front to back and bake for about 15 minutes more, until the lemons and dough are golden brown. Remove the focaccia from the pan, transfer to a wire rack, and cool for at least 10 minutes. Cut into squares and serve warm.

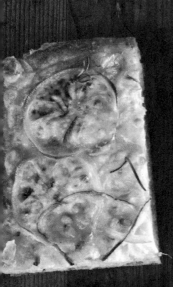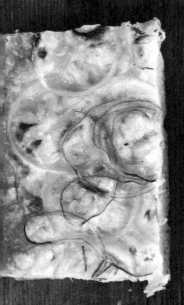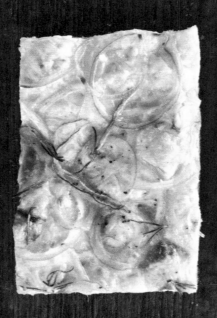

SALADS

SALAD WITHIN REACH

Sometimes less is still too much. That thought is always in the front of my mind when I'm making a salad. To me, a beautiful salad is all about restraint. It's about respecting and understanding the ingredients, and about letting them shine. If I had to share just one thing to give a person real tools for cooking, it would be how to prepare a salad. And that is all embodied in two words I always return to in all my cooking, but especially when thinking about salad: *optimal* and *appropriate*.

Optimal is pretty clear-cut. I use it to refer to food that is at its peak, its very best, because it's been nurtured with care in a landscape in which it can flourish, and harvested at a time dictated by its natural growing cycle. Optimal ingredients are those that are pretty much already perfect in the raw, so they offer the cook tremendous opportunities to play on that perfection, to shine a light on all the different qualities of the ingredient.

Appropriate is a little trickier. For me, *appropriate* as an adjective refers to things that are right in their context, that are in balance—like an appropriate amount of dressing for a salad, or an appropriate pairing of ingredients. And when I use the word as a verb, I don't think about it in its more negative connotation, of taking something that isn't mine, but rather as snatching up an optimal ingredient and exploiting all its amazing potential.

Making a salad can be a tremendous lesson in flavor, texture, and using what's on hand, and in considering the source— understanding where something comes

from—as well as what it is and how to handle it. Ideally you'd never make salad by going to the grocery store, recipe in hand. Instead, you'd hit the farmers' market and let what was best and fresh call to you. A salad within reach. A salad inspired by the season and the best available ingredients, not one dictated by a predetermined recipe, regardless of what makes sense.

Sometimes there is a very narrow window when an ingredient is at its optimum. In Arizona, we have a peach called Desert Gold, which usually comes into season in the last week of May, when the temperature goes from beautiful to hot as hell. When they are übersweet and warm from the sun, these peaches taste like peach cobbler straight off the tree. They are so ripe and vulnerable to bruising and bursting. When they are in season, I lay hands on as many as I can get and eat ridiculous amounts of them. The juices just run down my chin, and I let them—they are perfection. And yeah, you can't improve on perfection, but perfection is an opportunity. It gets me thinking, *How can I share this beautiful fruit? How can I showcase it? How can I make use of it in as many ways as possible while respecting this perfection?*

So here I am. I have a basket of fresh-picked Desert Golds. And I remember that my farmer has just delivered some young arugula. Now I have two flavor elements, sweet and bitter, and two textural elements, juicy and tender. I start thinking about a third ingredient. I reach for some fantastic goat cheese, a fatty and tangy element to add to the salad.

I take a few peaches, reserving the juiciest one, and pull them gently off the pits, tearing them apart over a bowl, because that juice is going to become a part of the dressing. Then, using my hand as a measure, I add arugula. I'm aiming for an equal proportion of fruit to green, so neither overpowers the other. I add the cheese to the arugula, the peaches, and their juices, and fold the salad gently with my hands so the cheese will find its way through the leaves and cling to some of them, its creamy whiteness just peeking through.

Dressing time. Dressing is there to enhance, not drown, the salad. So we're talking about an appropriate amount of olive oil. To me, that means that the leaves are just lightly coated in oil. After the olive oil, I reach for that juicy peach I set aside (I like to call it the sacrificial peach) and I just squeeze it over the salad. The juice that comes out provides a little extra acidity, sweetness, and balance. Using my hands again, I gently toss the salad with the dressing. And taste it. It will tell me what it needs. Does it need more oil? Does it need acidity? I might add just a dash of cider vinegar for brightness. When I tilt the plate holding my freshly dressed salad, there

is just a little juice and oil running gently out at the edges. Then I sprinkle some sea salt and freshly ground pepper over the top.

Finally, I realize the salad needs just one more ingredient to set off the juicy peaches, the tender greens, the silky cheese—it needs an element of contrast, with a texture and flavor that makes everything else pop. What else is in the kitchen? In Arizona, we get big, meaty pecans, and I have a fresh stash. So I grab some of them—a savory, woody element with a toothsome, oily texture.

So we've got bitter, sweet, slightly sour, clean, and fresh with just four ingredients.

I take the pecans and quickly warm them in a pan. I may add a drizzle of canola oil or a knob of butter, and I salt them too. Then I take the warmed pecans and give them a little "push" with a small hammer or the side of a bottle. I want broken pieces, not crumbs. I scatter them over the top of the salad.

And here it is. Perfect.

SIMPLE GREEN SALAD

Years ago, I read a great old American cookbook from the 1920s or '30s. It was a true relic of its time and place, of a small Midwestern town and its no-nonsense farmwives. My favorite recipe in the book was for boiled corn. It instructed the cook to set a pot of water to boil on the stove, walk out to the cornfield and pick several ears of corn with bright green husks and dark brown silk, then return to the kitchen, husk the ears, pop them into the boiling water, and pull them out as soon as the water returned to a boil. Happy days. The focus wasn't so much on all the things you might do with the corn as on how to pick the best corn and simply cook it optimally— set the water to boiling before you even leave the house, because sweet corn starts losing its flavor the moment it's picked. I love that mentality. Here all you have to do is find the most beautiful salad leaves and dry them thoroughly after rinsing so dressing won't just slide off them.

You wouldn't get out of the shower and put on your clothes without drying off first, right? Salads don't like getting dressed when they're wet either. Oil does not get along with water. The drier your salad leaves, the better your dressing will cling to them. I think about this in terms of making salads "waterproof." After you rinse your leaves and give them a few good spins in a salad spinner, spread them out on a clean kitchen towel and let them air-dry for a bit.

Then you add the appropriate amount of dressing: It's all about hitting that gentle balance where the dressing is in service to the greens— amplifying them rather than masking them. You have a role in composing the salad, but its parts, if well chosen, will already be perfect. Go to the farmers' market (or your own garden) and choose what's in season: a handful of springy bitter frisée, or some peppery mizuna, or tender, ruffly leaf lettuce, in combination or alone.

Serves 1

3 ounces mixed salad greens—the freshest and most local you can get—washed and dried

About 2 tablespoons Balsamic Dressing (recipe follows)

Fine sea salt and freshly ground black pepper

Just before you're ready to serve the salad, put your clean, dry leaves in a nice big bowl. Add the dressing—just enough to lightly coat the leaves. Gently toss the leaves with your hands, lightly glossing them with dressing. Sprinkle a little salt over the leaves and then add a turn or two of black pepper. Gently toss the leaves again. Taste for seasoning and add more salt or pepper if you'd like.

BALSAMIC DRESSING

Makes about ¾ cup

1 tablespoon honey
¼ cup balsamic vinegar
½ cup extra virgin olive oil

Fine sea salt and freshly ground black pepper

STABILITY

When I make dressing, I set a damp kitchen towel on my counter and nestle the bowl I'm going to use into the towel, so that it doesn't get crazy while I'm emulsifying the dressing. Stability!

Set a damp kitchen towel on your counter and place a small bowl on it, nestling the towel around the bowl to stabilize it. Pour in the honey, then slowly add the balsamic vinegar, whisking to incorporate it. Still whisking, slowly drizzle in the olive oil, whisking until the dressing is beautifully emulsified— nice and thick. Add a little salt and a few turns of pepper and taste the dressing. Good to go? Great. Want a little more salt or pepper? Go for it.

Stored in an airtight container, the dressing will keep for up to 2 weeks in the fridge.

PURSLANE AND CUCUMBER SALAD

Back in the early '90s, I was living in Santa Fe, working at the restaurant Babbo Ganzo. At the end of one summer, I was trying to think up a daily salad special. It was late in the season and I wasn't feeling especially fresh with ideas. I figured I'd drive out to the farmers' market and make a go of it. But Rocky, one of the kitchen crew, who had grown up in Sinaloa, Mexico, told me that there was tons of verdolaga growing between the sidewalk and the side of the building, poking through the cracks.

I had no idea what verdolaga was—turns out, it was purslane. But I'd never had purslane, or even known what it was. We picked a huge bag of it and Rocky told me how they prepared it back home. He shared his history with me, and my part was to be humble before that. We ended up making a simple purslane, cucumber, and red onion salad, dressed with a bit of lemon. Now purslane is one of my favorite greens; I love its sour lemony quality, its slipperiness. But back then, I had been ready to ignore the bounty that was right in front of me—and I think that's true too often for all of us, not only in cooking but in life.

I keep this salad simple—to give an ingredient that will be unfamiliar to many the opportunity to stand out. I also make sure that the salad plates are cool, that the cucumbers still have a chill on them, and that the purslane and onion are room temp. Temperature, like texture, is one of those invisible "ingredients" that can make or break a dish. If everything is the same temperature, the result is a disappointing homogeneity in your mouth.

PURSLANE

Most Americans, if they know it at all, know purslane mostly as a weed. But in the last few years, it's become more common at farmers' markets, and I couldn't be happier about that. Not only is purslane a crazy powerhouse of flavor, but it's also insanely nutritious. Among other things, it's full of an essential omega-3 fatty acid called alpha-linolenic acid (ALA) that helps prevent heart disease and is believed to reduce the risk for some cancers. The thing I like most about purslane, though, is its singular texture—it's slippery, almost like okra, when you bite into it. This quality makes it interesting to play with in other salads, like the Watermelon, Fennel, and Parsley Salad (page 55), where the absence of fat is an opportunity to highlight the unique mouthfeel of this often overlooked green; simply add some torn purslane to give the salad another dimension.

Serves 4

About 2 cups purslane leaves and tender stems, torn into bite-size pieces

¼ cup thin half-moon slices red onion

About 1 cup medium-thick half-moon slices cucumber (in a perfect world, unpeeled lemon or Armenian cucumbers or peeled English cucumbers)

2 to 3 tablespoons Simple Lemon Dressing (recipe follows)

Fine sea salt and freshly ground black pepper

A pinch of dried oregano, preferably wild (optional)

Combine the purslane, red onion, and cucumber in a large bowl. Add enough dressing to lightly coat the ingredients and gently toss with your hands. Sprinkle on a touch of salt, add a turn of pepper, and gently mix again. If you have it on hand, sprinkle on the oregano, bruising it between your fingers as you add it.

SIMPLE LEMON DRESSING

Makes ¾ cup

¼ cup fresh lemon juice
½ cup extra virgin olive oil
Fine sea salt

Set a damp kitchen towel on your counter and place a medium bowl on it, nestling the towel around the bowl to stabilize it. Pour in the lemon juice and then, whisking, slowly add the oil, whisking until the dressing is emulsified—nice and thick. Add a pinch of salt and give it a whisk, then taste and add another pinch of salt if you want.

Stored in an airtight container, the dressing will keep for up to 2 weeks in the fridge.

SUNDAY SALAD (ESCAROLE SALAD)

Salad wasn't always part of the meal when I was growing up; my mother would serve vegetables as a side, but salad wasn't a thing in our house. When I was about ten, though, my grandfather and uncles built a cabin upstate, in Pinebush, New York, where my grandfather planted a beautiful garden. We started going up there on the weekends, and on Sundays we'd have a big dinner and my grandfather would make a salad with romaine and red onion yanked straight from his garden, homemade red wine vinegar, and some nothing-fancy olive oil. Everything about the garden felt exotic, and my grandfather's salad seemed part of that too. This salad is the grown-up translation of that memory. The beauty of escarole hearts is that they're crunchy without being watery, and they recall the slight licorice note of romaine but with a clean, pleasantly bitter edge. The oregano is critical to the magic; its heady, medicinal scent is like a Fellini film come to life, or maybe an old-school Italian social club.

Serves 4

1 head escarole, outer leaves removed
A generous slice of pain au levain or
    sourdough bread
1 garlic clove, halved
Extra virgin olive oil, for drizzling
8 thin slices red onion
¼ cup Cider Vinegar Dressing
    (page 50)

Fine sea salt and freshly ground black
    pepper
A couple of good pinches of dried
    oregano, preferably wild
1 ounce blue cheese (I use a great
    Stilton or Gorgonzola, or Point Reyes
    Blue from Northern California),
    crumbled

To toast the bread: Preheat the oven to 350°F or, even better, heat an outdoor grill (you could also toast the bread on a hot grill pan on the stovetop).

Meanwhile, separate the escarole leaves and wash and dry them thoroughly. I like to trim about ⅓ inch off the tops, as the pointy ends of the leaves can sometimes be bitter. Grab a big bowl and tear the leaves into about 1-inch-wide strips, dropping them into the bowl.

Now lay the bread directly on the oven rack or on the grill (or in the grill pan) and toast until crisp, a couple of minutes. It's nice to get a few char lines on the slice, a little hint of burnt toast. Remove the bread from the heat and rub it all over with one of the garlic clove halves, then drizzle it with some olive oil. Tear the bread into rough pieces and set aside.

Add the onion slices to the bowl of escarole, then add the dressing and mix gently with your hands so that the dressing evenly coats the greens. Add a sprinkle of salt and a couple of turns of pepper, then add the oregano, pinching it with your fingers as you do so to release all that heady scent (I call this "activating" it), and mix one last time.

Carefully divide the salad among four plates and finish each serving with a few pieces of torn bread and some of the blue cheese.

CIDER VINEGAR DRESSING

Makes about 1 cup

2 teaspoons honey
¼ cup apple cider vinegar
¾ cup extra virgin olive oil

Fine sea salt and freshly ground black
  pepper

Set a damp kitchen towel on your counter and place a medium bowl on it, nestling the towel around the bowl to stabilize it. Pour the honey into the bowl, then slowly add the vinegar, whisking to incorporate it. Still whisking, slowly drizzle in the olive oil, whisking until the dressing is beautifully emulsified—nice and thick. Add a little sea salt and a few turns of pepper. Taste the dressing and add a little more salt or pepper if you like.

Stored in an airtight container, the dressing will keep for up to 2 weeks in the fridge.

FENNEL AND BLOOD ORANGE SALAD

This salad is bright and full of flavor—sunshine on your plate, even in a hard winter. I love blood oranges and look forward to December, when they start showing up at the market, but any good citrus will work. Grapefruit would be especially nice here (if you are using it, you want the fruit to be heavy and ripe—and maybe one of the pink or red varietals; you'll need two grapefruits). But citrus requires a different strategy for the dressing: Where watermelon has almost no acidity, blood oranges are about 80 percent acid. So, to bring this salad into balance, you need to gloss the fruit with a little fat—olive oil—to take it down to a place of about 50 percent acidity.

Fennel changes over the year too. In summer, it is mature and the bulbs are big and hearty—the perfect partner to crystalline watermelon. But in winter and spring, tender baby fennel bulbs are the perfect foil for the juicy tenderness of the citrus segments. I like to slice these guys into ribbons with a mandoline; the little curls emphasize their delicacy. I keep the parsley leaves whole, so you taste them as an integral part of the salad, not simply a garnish.

We get bee pollen from the same farm where we source honey (as well as the citrus and the fennel), and we lightly dust this salad with it. It adds just a hint of sweetness. If you don't have bee pollen, a drizzle of good honey will be just as delicious.

Serves 4

8 baby fennel bulbs or 4 small fennel bulbs, trimmed
4 blood oranges, peeled
¼ cup loosely packed fresh flat-leaf parsley leaves
Juice of 2 oranges

1 teaspoon extra virgin olive oil
Fine sea salt and freshly ground black pepper
1 teaspoon bee pollen, or good honey for drizzling

Thinly slice the fennel bulbs crosswise on a mandoline (mind your fingers) and put them in a large bowl. Or, if you don't have a mandoline, slice the fennel as thin as you can, aiming for paper-thin ribbons.

Using a very sharp knife, slice the blood oranges into rounds ⅓ to ½ inch thick. Add the orange slices to the bowl of fennel, then add the parsley.

Pour the orange juice over the salad, drizzle on the olive oil, and sprinkle with salt and pepper to taste. Use your hands to gently combine the ingredients, making sure everything has a nice gloss of juice and oil.

Divide the salad among four plates and finish each one with a light dusting of bee pollen or a drizzle of honey.

WATERMELON, FENNEL, AND PARSLEY SALAD

On a hot summer day—and it gets *really* hot here in Arizona—when I can barely think about eating, much less getting in front of a stove, this salad is everything I want in a plate of food. Fresh and sweet and cool, it is satisfyingly toothsome but light. The parsley balances the flavors of the watermelon and fennel, so it's not a fight between licorice and sweet, and black pepper brings heat. Since watermelon has almost zero acidity, the lemon adds a tart clarity that brightens the whole dish. At home, when I'm answering only to my own mood or the whims of my family, I treat the salad as more of a rough composition, and so should you. If you want more of that anise-y crunch, add more fennel. This is another salad in which temperature is a crucial "ingredient." Make sure the watermelon is as chilled as possible, the fennel is cool but not cold, and the parsley is room temp, so all its herbaceous greenness comes through.

Note: There is no oil in this salad. The juice reminds me of a great cocktail. The juice at the end—that tells you all you need to know.

Serves 4

One 3-pound seedless watermelon, rind removed and cut into large chunks
Juice of 3 lemons
1 small fennel bulb, trimmed and thinly sliced

¼ cup loosely packed fresh flat-leaf parsley leaves
Fine sea salt and freshly ground black pepper

To make the dressing: Put about ¾ pound (4 cups) of the watermelon cubes in a blender or food processor and pulse one or two times, just until you have what looks like a slurry of melon and juice, then add the lemon juice and give it another quick pulse. The key is to just get a nice mix of watermelon liquid and lemon juice. It will look very loose. Put it through a strainer and set it aside.

Combine the remaining watermelon chunks, the fennel, and parsley in a large bowl and season with salt and pepper. Give everything just a gentle mix by hand, so as not to break up the watermelon.

Slowly pour most of the watermelon dressing over the salad and mix gently to combine. Divide the salad among four plates and spoon a little of the remaining dressing over each.

PANZANELLA

It is strange to me that bread is so often treated as an afterthought or an extender, instead of the star it can be—especially now that so many places have amazing artisanal bakeries doing all kinds of beautiful, rustic loaves. Let's say you've got one of those loaves at home right now, but for whatever reason, you didn't eat it all right away and now it's a couple of days old: Panzanella is an opportunity to revitalize that bread, to use its texture—its dryness or slight toughness—as a springboard for a different approach that still takes advantage of its inherent deliciousness.

Or let's say you have a fresh loaf on hand, and it's a beautiful summer day and you're grilling a T-bone. You've already prepared the fire for the steak, and you realize that the smoke and heat of that fire will do wonders for that great country bread as well.

At the heart of panzanella are thick slices of grilled bread, rubbed with garlic, lashed with fruity oil, and married with juicy tomatoes and crunchy cucumbers. It's the perfect dish for an easy two-course meal, because it combines vegetables and starch in one go. This is a great opportunity to use beautiful but misshapen tomatoes, be they Green Zebra or Black Prince or whatever killer tomato works for you. Look for different varieties of cucumber too, such as Kirby, Persian, or English. If you have some of these growing in your garden, the bumpy, funny-looking ones or curly ones are fine—it's flavor you're after here, not looks.

Serves 4

2 large ripe tomatoes
About ¾ pound cucumbers, preferably
  an assortment (see headnote)
1 small red onion
3 big slices rustic bread
1 garlic clove, halved
½ cup extra virgin olive oil, plus more
  for drizzling

Fine sea salt
1 teaspoon dried oregano, preferably
  wild
¼ cup red wine vinegar
Freshly ground black pepper

Get an outdoor grill good and hot or preheat the oven to 400°F.

Meanwhile, roughly chop the tomatoes and add them, with their juices, to a large salad bowl. Halve the cucumbers lengthwise, then slice them crosswise into thin half-moons. Add to the tomatoes. Halve the red onion lengthwise and slice it into thin half-moons as well. Add to the bowl.

When the grill or oven is ready, toast the bread, turning once, until golden on both sides. While the bread is still warm, rub the cut sides of the garlic over both sides of the bread's raspy surface. Set the bread on a cutting board or plate and lash both sides with a few good passes of olive oil. Sprinkle lightly with salt and then with the oregano, pinching the herb with your fingers to release all that heady scent.

Tear the bread straight into the salad bowl, in rough pieces that aren't too large but make for a substantial bite. Give everything a good toss to combine. Add the ½ cup olive oil to the bowl, pouring it evenly over the bread and vegetables. Do the same with the vinegar, then season with salt and pepper, remembering that the bread is already seasoned. Give everything a good but gentle stir to mix and taste for seasoning. Add a little kiss of extra seasoning if necessary.

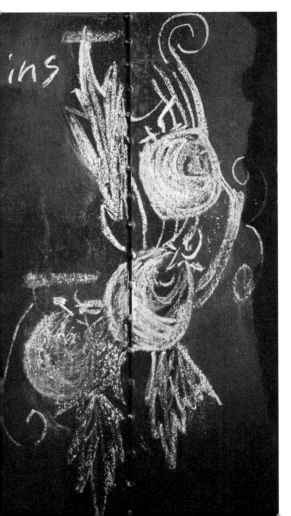

BRUSSELS SPROUTS SLAW

The ever-polarizing Brussels sprouts only bring me a smile. Certain cooking methods—stewing, braising, anything low-and-slow—are more common in winter because tougher, heartier winter vegetables need more time, and that is how I usually cook Brussels sprouts, long and gently, Italian-style, with maybe a little pancetta and a little chile in the mix. But sometimes I want some fresh, raw vegetable crunch in my life during a long winter. The key here is slicing the sprouts as thin as possible. When the leaves are transformed into little ribbons, they manage to hold on to all their great brassica brashness but also really absorb the smoky saltiness of the bacon, the sweetness of the honey mustard, and the sharpness of the red onion. The acid in the dressing helps make the raw sprouts more digestible, even as they retain their pleasing crunch.

Serves 4

A couple of slices thick-cut smoked
　　bacon
¾ pound Brussels sprouts (about
　　12 medium sprouts), trimmed
¼ red onion, thinly sliced

¼ cup **Honey Mustard Dressing**
　　(page 60), or to taste
Fine sea salt (optional)
Freshly ground black pepper

Lay the bacon in a cold skillet and set it over medium-low heat. The bacon will start releasing its fat into the pan and then it will begin to curl and buckle a little. Once it does, grab some tongs, flip the bacon, and continue to cook until it's a little crispy but still tender, flipping it every now and then.

Meanwhile, halve the sprouts lengthwise, then lay them flat and slice crosswise into ribbons. Put the sprouts in a bowl.

When the bacon is ready, remove it from the pan, slice it into strips about ⅓ inch wide, and immediately add them to the sprouts (the warm bacon will continue to release some fat, and you want that delicious fat in your salad, not on your cutting board). Gently mix the sprouts and bacon together. The warm fat will also wilt the ribboned sprouts slightly, giving the salad a beautiful silky texture.

Mix in the red onion, then add the dressing and gently toss everything together. Taste, and season the salad with salt if it needs it (the bacon will give the salad a nice hit of salinity) and about 4 good turns of pepper.

HONEY MUSTARD DRESSING

Makes about 1 cup

2 teaspoons whole-grain mustard
2 teaspoons honey, preferably local
¼ cup apple cider vinegar

¾ cup extra virgin olive oil
Fine sea salt and freshly ground black
   pepper

Set a damp kitchen towel on your counter and place a medium bowl on it, nestling the towel around the bowl to stabilize it. Add the mustard and honey to the bowl and whisk together. Slowly add the apple cider vinegar, whisking as you do so. Still whisking, slowly drizzle in the olive oil and whisk until the dressing is beautifully emulsified—nice and thick. Add a little sea salt and a few turns of pepper and taste the dressing. If you want a little more salt or pepper, go for it.

Stored in an airtight container, the dressing will keep for up to 2 weeks in the fridge.

WARM CABBAGE SALAD WITH APPLES AND BLUE CHEESE

Caraway is, for me, one of those transporting flavors. The slightest hint of it calls to mind some of life's great pleasures: sauerkraut, a perfect Reuben sandwich, and, especially, real Jewish rye. Before I left New York, there were three breads in my life: the crusty, airy Italian bread we ate at home; flavorless, squishy Wonder Bread; and—ah—Jewish rye. I loved the chew of it, the texture. It was the opposite of Wonder Bread in every way, and it was also totally different from Italian bread: It was dense, without any big holes, and it had seeds in it. I loved the aromatic headiness of

the caraway seeds when you toasted a slice. There was something Old World about the caraway, exotic but comforting and warming.

So the first time I encountered caraway in Italy, I was surprised and then not surprised. I was in a restaurant in Friuli, in northernmost Italy, on the border of the Alps, where the Austrian influence runs deep. The dish was stewed cabbage with caraway, super earthy, and I loved the somehow familiar but new combination of flavors. This warm salad—the cabbage is less cooked down, more textural—is both my riff on that Italo-Austrian dish and an homage to the Jewish rye of my childhood. It's a heady salad, one that should take you places. To me, it tastes of the Alps, somewhere cold and sharp, with that mountainy blue cheese, strong and bloomy, almost piney.

Because this is a warm salad, you don't want to prepare it ahead of time, or it will get soggy. Make it just before you serve it.

Serves 2

2 tablespoons extra virgin olive oil,
  plus a little for the walnuts
1 teaspoon caraway seeds
About ½ pound red cabbage (¼ head),
  thinly sliced
About ½ pound Savoy cabbage
  (¼ head), thinly sliced
½ red onion, thinly sliced
Fine sea salt and freshly ground black
  pepper

¾ cup walnuts
1 apple, peeled, cored, and cut into
  rough chunks
¼ cup Cider Vinegar Dressing
  (page 50)
¼ cup vegetable stock
¼ pound blue cheese (I use a great
  Stilton or Gorgonzola, or Point Reyes
  Blue from Northern California)

Preheat the oven to 350°F.

You want to use a nice big skillet for the cabbage so that it won't actually braise when you add the dressing and stock (a larger pan means greater surface area, which means less depth of liquid, so less of the cabbage will be immersed—and the liquid will also reduce more quickly).

Set the pan over medium heat and add the olive oil. After a minute or so, when the oil is hot but not rippling, add the caraway seeds and toast them for about 15 seconds. The seeds should give off a very floral fragrance, but be careful not to burn them—as soon they're aromatic, add the cabbage and red onion. Give everything a stir, season with salt and pepper, and cook, stirring occasionally, until the vegetables are just wilted, 2 to 3 minutes.

Meanwhile, spread the walnuts out on a baking sheet, give them a light gloss of olive oil, and sprinkle with salt. Pop them into the oven for 5 minutes or so, until they are nice and crunchy. Spread the toasted nuts out on a cutting board and crush them roughly with the back of a knife or the bottom of a pan.

Once the cabbage is wilted, add the apples to the pan and sauté until they have taken on some color, a minute or so. Increase the heat to high and add the dressing, stirring with a wooden spoon to deglaze the pan. When the liquid is reduced by about two-thirds, add the vegetable stock and cook, stirring to prevent sticking, until the liquid is again reduced by about two-thirds. Remove the pan from the heat.

Add the toasted walnuts to the cabbage and crumble in the blue cheese. Toss gently to incorporate.

Divide the salad between two plates. Spoon any liquid left in the pan over the salad and serve immediately.

POTATO SALAD

Potato salad has a lot in common with an often underrated favorite of mine, panzanella (see page 56), in that it's made with a humble, inexpensive, filling ingredient. The truth is, though, growing up I was never crazy about potato salad: *so much mayonnaise.* Way too much. To me, potato salad was a bland mayonnaise-fueled carb-bomb—until I had German potato salad for the first time. I do remember how weirded out I was by this no-mayo potato salad. But it was delicious—acidic with vinegar, salty with bacon fat, silky with oil. The potato salad here is both my take on that salad and my nod—hey, pickles—to the American classic.

Serves 6

2 pounds medium-starch potatoes, such as Yukon Gold or German Butterball (6 to 8 potatoes)
Fine sea salt
2 bay leaves, preferably fresh
One 14-ounce jar sweet pickles, drained, juice reserved
¾ cup Gaeta or Kalamata olives, pitted and chopped
1 tablespoon Dijon mustard
8 spring onions or large scallions, chopped
A handful of chopped fresh flat-leaf parsley
1 tablespoon dried oregano, preferably wild
2 tablespoons white wine vinegar

Put the potatoes in a large pot with enough water to cover them by 2 inches or so, bring to a boil over high heat, and add 1 teaspoon salt and the bay leaves. Reduce the heat to a gentle boil and cook, uncovered, until the potatoes are tender when pierced with a knife, about 30 minutes.

Meanwhile, make the dressing (the potatoes should still be warm when they hit the dressing; this is the secret to their really absorbing the dressing's flavor). Chop the pickles into medium dice and put them in a large bowl (this bowl is what you'll use to mix and serve the salad). Add the reserved pickle juice, the olives, mustard, onions or scallions, parsley, oregano (pinching it with your fingers to release all that heady scent), and vinegar and mix well.

When the potatoes are ready, drain them in a colander and let cool just enough so that you can handle them. Then cut them into quarters, letting them drop directly into the bowl of dressing. Gently mix everything together and let the flavors marry for at least a few minutes.

Serve warm or at room temperature.

SANDWICHES

MOZZARELLA AND TOMATO SANDWICH	73
ROASTED TOMATO AND GOAT CHEESE SANDWICH	75
FRITTATA SANDWICH	77
TUNA SALAD SANDWICH	80
SOPPRESSATA AND PROVOLONE SANDWICH	83
THE MEATBALL HERO	85
PULLED LAMB SANDWICH	90

CONSIDER THE SANDWICH

There are few foods simpler than the sandwich, and yet it is so full of potential for showing how intentional, attention-driven cooking can yield a whole so much greater than the sum of its parts (though it should, of course, always start with the most optimal parts). Many of us eat a sandwich every single day. Sandwiches are the ultimate peoples' food. They're democratic. They're usually pretty affordable.

Because they are portable, they're perfect for both working folks and schoolkids. They don't require a ton of kitchen know-how or even many tools beyond a knife. But in their very *everydayness*, they are the kind of food that we take for granted and may, for that reason, find ourselves eating even when they're not very good, which is often: Gluey bread with no taste or texture. Sad, limp lettuce that acts as a slip 'n' slide for everything else inside, shooting pickles and tomatoes onto your lap. Over-refrigerated rubbery meat that seems to have come from outer space. Even processed cheese.

But sandwiches deserve so much better. Precisely because they are humble and unassuming, sandwiches have a lot to teach us about what it takes to make good food. Most people are rarely

prepared to answer the question of why they think a certain food is good (or why it's not), and just taking the time to ask that question is the beginning of a great sandwich, or of any good cooking experience.

For a lot of us, texture is the first thing we recognize when thinking of why we like or hate a particular food. Is there a bigger letdown than a mealy apple or a soggy potato chip? Every food and every component of a dish has an ideal texture, one that best enhances its flavor. In cooking, we combine those textures and those flavors for maximum effect. We want that apple to be crisp, right? We want the taut skin to yield to a juicy, sweet-tart bite, the crispness of the flesh and the brightness of the flavor amplifying each other just so. Sandwiches are an object lesson in how elemental texture is when it comes to joy in food. There's nowhere to hide when it comes to the sandwich—all of its components have to play well together.

So the best sandwiches, as with any foods, happen when you strive to be clear on what you like—or what the people you are cooking for like—and to figure out how to get there, and what you need, given the context. This is why I love making sandwiches for other people, because it is the ultimate opportunity to practice listening and then executing based on their preferences. In fact, a few years ago, for a couple of minutes, I thought it would be genius to do an entire book—*The Architecture of the Sandwich*—interviewing some of the world's greatest architects about the type of sandwiches they would build. I gave up on that pretty quickly, but the principle still holds for me: A good architect builds a home to suit the needs—physical and emotional—of its inhabitants. When you build a sandwich, you should be arming yourself with that same kind of intention and attention—being thoughtful and present. Who are you making the sandwich for? (If it's for a three-year-old, for example, you might want to cut off the crusts.) Then determine when they are going to eat it. If it won't be for several hours, you need to be thoughtful about the order in which you layer the ingredients, using the cheese or meat or another fatty ingredient to insulate the bread against any juicy vegetables. Where are they going to eat it? If it's at a table, great. Go crazy with a saucy meatball hero. Or on a quick lunch break? A tidy salami and provolone sandwich makes more sense.

With the sandwiches in this chapter, I want to arm you with the idea that, no matter what you make, you need to draw on all the sensibilities you already have. Show up for yourself and the people you're feeding, be present in front of the stove or the cutting board or the fridge. It's almost never about already knowing the answer; it's about remembering to ask the question. What makes good things good for me (or you), and for now?

Market Sandwiches

Monday	Mozzarella, Prosciutto, Basil
Tuesday	Roasted tomato, Arugula, Goat cheese
Wednesday	Mortadella, Sweet & spicy tomato Jam, Manchego
Thursday	Sloppy Giuseppe
Friday	Bacon, Fontina, tomato
Saturday	Shriners Sausage, Roasted onions
Sunday	Egg Frittata

BREAD

At Pane Bianco, we build all of our sandwiches on our own focaccia (my brother, Marco, and our team make all the bread for our restaurants, and it is amazing). You can follow suit at home, or you can use any great bread that's sturdy but yielding, like ciabatta or a crusty pane Pugliese. When you're making a sandwich, you want to think of the bread as an equal partner to the filling. The two are costars: They should have good chemistry and make sense together. Think of how the earthiness of a coarse multigrain helps bring out the greenness of sprouts and avocado in that classic veggie sandwich, or how dense, caraway-flecked Jewish rye is the natural partner for the luscious fattiness of pastrami. When I build a sandwich, I also like to think of the bread as a cradle for the ingredients—so I often tear out a bit of the insides, the better for holding the ingredients and keeping everything from dancing when you bite down. If you're making more than a sandwich or two, save the pieces of torn-out bread for bread crumbs, or fry them up in a little olive oil for rustic croutons.

MOZZARELLA AND TOMATO SANDWICH

One bite of this sandwich, a Caprese salad between slices of bread, should transport you to the sun-soaked isle of Capri in the summertime, when everything is perfect: the tomatoes hanging heavy in the vine, so ripe you can smell them, and the basil deep green and fragrant. It's the kind of sandwich you make only when your produce is absolutely right, when market tables are loaded with beautiful, juicy tomatoes and fresh herbs. And then there is the fresh mozzarella and great olive oil. In short, this sandwich is about the assembling of fat and sweet and acid. And it is a great chance to discover what olive oils you like best. Maybe you like a grassier olive oil, maybe you like a fruitier one.

But the sandwich is not just about great ingredients—you need great ingredients *at the right temperature.* Your tomatoes should feel warm from the sun—or at least as warm as your room. The mozzarella should be almost but not quite at room temperature—it shouldn't have a chill on it, but it should still have just a hint of coolness. This way, the tomatoes and the cheese play off each other, the different temperatures underscoring their textures and flavors and aromas. Because the ripe tomato will release liquid, you want to use a bread that's fairly sturdy, like focaccia.

I love that this sandwich is a great starting place for people learning to make pizza. These are the key ingredients they'll be working with, but in raw form. At its most elemental, pizza starts with tomato, mozzarella, and basil. And it's also a great lesson in sourcing.

Makes 1 sandwich

A piece of ciabatta, a hunk of crusty
    bread, or 1 large piece Focaccia
    (page 33), split in half
4 medium-thick slices ripe, juicy
    tomato (about 1 small)
3 ounces fresh mozzarella, thickly
    sliced

3 or 4 fresh basil leaves
Extra virgin olive oil, for drizzling
Fine sea salt and freshly ground black
    pepper

This sandwich is all about balancing the layers so you get a bite of sweet-acidic tomato and milky mozzarella every time, without any runaways making a dash for your lap. Take one of the halves of your bread and tear out just a little of the insides, making a very shallow cradle for the tomatoes. Gently lay the tomato slices on that half of bread, overlapping them slightly if need be. (You add the tomatoes first so the bread can absorb some of their delicious juices.) Lay the sliced mozzarella over the tomatoes. Add the basil, tearing any really big leaves (so you don't pull a whole one out in one bite), scattering them over the mozzarella. The basil adds a little texture, a little pepperiness, and its scent— which is something like that of the stem of the tomato.

Give the sandwich a drizzle of extra virgin olive oil and season with a pinch of salt and a few turns of cracked pepper. Top with the other half of the bread. I like to slice the sandwich in half on the diagonal for a nice visual, and because it makes it easier to eat, but dig right in if that's where you're at.

ROASTED TOMATO AND GOAT CHEESE SANDWICH

Here we have another riff on the holy tomato and cheese combo, building on the idea of the Mozzarella and Tomato Sandwich (page 73). But where that guy is all about almost-untouched ingredients, this iteration is transformed by the simple element of heat. Instead of super-bright and -juicy fresh tomatoes, these are sweetly concentrated oven-roasted tomatoes, spiked with wild oregano. And instead of milky mozzarella, there is tart, creamy goat cheese, which can stand up to the robust flavor of the roasted tomatoes. All the building blocks that make that first sandwich a great one are still here: texture, acidity, and fat. Same basic elements, different approaches. Here the herb is parsley, not basil, and it is used more generously. The fresh greenness of the parsley is a nice foil for the peppery arugula, the sweetly acidic tomatoes, and the creamy cheese. It's a clean, cool flavor that brings everything together.

Once you've enjoyed both these sandwiches, let yourself play. You can change the acidity, the fat, the textures. And, having learned the "architecture" of a good sandwich, you can begin to expand your ambitions.

Makes 1 sandwich

A piece of ciabatta, a hunk of crusty
  bread, or 1 large piece Focaccia
  (page 33), split in half
2 ounces chèvre or cow's milk cheese
  or Brie

(ingredients continue on next page)

Freshly ground black pepper
Extra virgin olive oil, for drizzling
About ⅓ cup Roasted Tomatoes with
    Wild Oregano (page 154)
¾ cup loosely packed arugula

1 tablespoon Balsamic Dressing
    (page 45)
About 2 tablespoons fresh flat-leaf
    parsley leaves

Take one of the halves of bread and spread it evenly with the chèvre.

Crank some pepper—as you much as you like—over the cheese, then give it all a few nice passes of olive oil. Spoon the roasted tomatoes evenly over the cheese. You want to get a little tomato, a little cheese in every bite you take.

Quickly toss the arugula with the dressing in a small bowl. (Do this now, not before you start making the sandwich, so the greens won't have the chance to wilt.) Top the tomatoes with the dressed greens and then sprinkle them with the parsley. Top the greens with the other half of the bread. Slice the sandwich in half on the diagonal.

FRITTATA SANDWICH

A pepper and egg sandwich is one of those New York deli classics you don't see much of west of the Hudson. When I was growing up, if you had $1.50 in your pocket, there you were: hard-scrambled eggs and a mess of frying peppers, cooked up in a, let's say, *generous* amount of olive oil, all piled on a squishy roll. It was sandwiches like that bad boy that gave me a love of breakfast for dinner, especially on one of those lazy Sundays where you get up late and time moves fast and slow all at once and before you know it, it's five p.m.—early, but you're ready for dinner. This frittata sandwich is a take on that old deli classic, equally humble and perfect for anytime, day or night, you want to put together something delicious without planning or shopping. The frittata is casual rustic—the kind of dish you can throw together from leftovers, something as good at room temp as it is hot. (Even so, use free-range eggs if you can, for their rich flavor and super-sunny orange yolks.) And when you slide the frittata onto a piece of hearty country bread or focaccia: instant meal. Just keep in mind that when you're making a frittata for a sandwich, you want it to be about the same size as the bread you are using. Here an 8-inch skillet should do the trick, and a well-seasoned cast-iron one is ideal.

Makes 1 sandwich

FOR THE FRITTATA

1 to 2 tablespoons extra virgin olive oil

1 ounce thinly sliced prosciutto, torn into strips or pieces

2 to 3 asparagus spears, cut into pieces, or ¼ onion (optional)

2 large eggs, preferably free-range

Fine sea salt and freshly ground black pepper

1 ounce Parmigiano-Reggiano, finely grated

FOR THE SANDWICH

A piece of ciabatta, a hunk of crusty bread, or 1 large piece Focaccia (page 33), split in half

Scant ½ cup Roasted Tomatoes with Wild Oregano (page 154)

A handful of salad greens of your choosing

1 tablespoon Balsamic Dressing (page 45)

Extra virgin olive oil, for drizzling

Fine sea salt

To make the frittata: Set an ovenproof 8-inch skillet (preferably cast-iron) over high heat and get it nice and hot. Add 1 tablespoon olive oil and let it get good and hot, but not smoking, then add the prosciutto. If you're using asparagus, add it now. You want the prosciutto to get a good crispness on it to stand up to the eggs. This should take about 2 minutes; stir the prosciutto occasionally so it doesn't stick.

Meanwhile, crack your eggs into a bowl and lightly beat them together. Season them with a good pinch of salt and a few twists of pepper, then give it all another quick whisk or two.

Set an oven rack just below the broiler and turn it on.

Make sure there's enough oil in the pan—you may need to add up to another tablespoon of oil so your pan has a nice even coating—and then slowly pour in the eggs. As the eggs cook, you want to nudge them a bit, to distribute the prosciutto throughout them—you don't want it all clumped up in the center. Cook the eggs for just a couple of minutes, until they are set on the bottom but still runny on top—you're going to finish the frittata under the broiler.

Scatter the Parmigiano evenly over the top of the frittata, then pop the pan under the broiler. Give it a couple of minutes so the cheese melts and the eggs fluff up. You don't want your eggs runny, but you don't want them dry either.

Grab an oven mitt, pull the frittata out of the oven, and let it rest for 30 seconds or so before you turn it out.

To assemble the sandwich: Gently center the frittata on one of the halves of bread and top it with the roasted tomatoes, arranging them evenly. Give the salad greens a quick toss with the vinaigrette in a small bowl and mound them on the tomatoes and eggs. Give the whole thing a healthy drizzle of olive oil, followed by a pinch of salt, and top with the other half of the bread. Slice the sandwich in half on the diagonal.

TUNA SALAD SANDWICH

Being in the desert, we don't do fresh fish at our restaurants, but when I was thinking about what kind of sandwiches to offer at Pane Bianco, my sandwich shop in north-central Phoenix, I knew I wanted to include a tuna sandwich. There were two reasons motivating me: The first was that a tuna salad sandwich is a classic, and I'm always thinking about how to revitalize a classic, how to shine a light on and elevate the qualities that make the dish enduring. The second was that I wanted to undermine people's tendency to order automatically, to order something that's a known quantity just because it's pretty much the same everywhere. I wanted to surprise my customers, to please them, of course, but also to give them a new way to think about tuna salad. For most of us, our expectations for tuna sandwiches are pretty low. When I was growing up in New York, tuna salad was served up in ice cream scoops, drowned in mayonnaise and icy-cold from the fridge. It felt processed. You didn't even really compute that it came from the sea. It wasn't vegetable, animal, or mineral, it was just . . . tuna. In this sandwich, I didn't want to lean on a monsoon of mayo—in fact, there's no mayo at all. Instead, it's crunchy and fresh with celery, salty, slightly sweet with raisins and apples, bright with lemon, and tart with vinegar—all brought together with the olive oil.

We get our tuna, one of the only nonlocal products we use, from a fishing and canning co-op in Seattle. The tuna is sustainably caught off the coast of Alaska by local fishermen. Increasingly, tuna is being overfished and netted in ways that damage the environment. A huge reason for this is the history of treating tuna, especially canned tuna, as a "less-than" product. At Pane Bianco, we want to correct that—and our tuna sandwich is the most expensive one on the menu.

Makes 1 sandwich

½ recipe Tuna Salad (recipe follows)
A piece of ciabatta, a hunk of crusty
   bread, or 1 large piece Focaccia
   (page 33), split in half

½ cup arugula
1 tablespoon Balsamic Dressing
   (page 45)
Extra virgin olive oil, for drizzling

Spoon the tuna onto one of the halves of bread and spread it out so it's
evenly distributed over the bread.

     Quickly toss the arugula with the balsamic dressing in a small bowl.
Top the tuna with the arugula and drizzle the whole thing with a little olive
oil. Cover with the second piece of bread. Slice the sandwich in half on the
diagonal.

TUNA SALAD

There's enough tuna salad here for two sandwiches—if you're making just
one for yourself, refrigerate the leftover tuna in an airtight container and use
it within a day.

Serves 2

One 5-ounce can high-quality tuna in
   olive oil (such as Wild Planet)
½ cup peeled, diced sweet-tart apple,
   such as Granny Smith or Fuji
¼ cup diced celery
4 Gaeta or Kalamata olives, pitted and
   chopped
1 tablespoon raisins, chopped

½ cup loosely packed chopped fresh
   flat-leaf parsley
¼ cup extra virgin olive oil
2 tablespoons red wine vinegar
Juice of 1 lemon
Fine sea salt and freshly ground black
   pepper

Flake the tuna, along with its liquid—I like it to be a little chunky—into a
medium bowl. Add the apple, celery, olives, raisins, parsley, oil, vinegar,
lemon juice, and salt and pepper to taste and mix until well incorporated.
Taste the tuna salad and season it with a little more salt and pepper if
you feel it needs it, then mix again. Cover and refrigerate if not using
immediately.

SOPPRESSATA AND PROVOLONE SANDWICH

When I was growing up in New York City, you could only really get four Italian cheeses: There were Parmesan and pecorino, for pasta and for seasoning food. There was mozzarella, for pizza, baked pastas, and antipasto platters. And there was provolone. Provolone was sharp and strong. It could stand up to the cured meats sitting right next to it in the deli case. It was *the* sandwich cheese. Open the lunch box of any working-class Italian dude in 1920s or '30s New York—like my grandfather, a train operator, a union guy, a tough guy—and you'd find a thermos of black coffee and, wrapped in wax paper, a greasy provolone and cured meat sandwich.

This sandwich is an exercise in capturing the nostalgia of that classic Italian deli sandwich but with a more balanced flavor profile. The soppressata adds its own pop of black pepper and coarse porky salinity. Provolone is an assertive cheese, and too much can obscure the other flavors. Here the roasted peppers bring a sweet, slippery quality and moisture to what would otherwise be a rather dry enterprise.

With this sandwich, the meat doesn't have to be soppressata. Trust your own taste: It could be any salami; it could be coppa, or perhaps even finocchiona. Some cured meats are drier than others, though, so think about that and use it as an opportunity to be intentional (think about what you're aiming for). Instead of the provolone, you could use another slightly sharp aged cheese, such as Asiago. Maybe you'll add another pass of olive oil when you finish the sandwich. Or maybe you'll decide on a few more peppers. Or forget the peppers and go for pickles. This sandwich is an opportunity to practice asking yourself, *What makes good things good, for me and for now?*

Makes 1 sandwich

A piece of ciabatta, a hunk of crusty bread, or 1 large piece Focaccia (page 33), split in half
2 ounces sliced soppressata

2 ounces sliced provolone
¼ cup Grilled Red Peppers (page 145)
Extra virgin olive oil, for drizzling

Tear out just a little of the insides of one of the halves of your bread, making a shallow cradle for the soppressata, provolone, and peppers. Lay the soppressata on the bread, covering the surface evenly, to insulate the bread against the peppers and their juices. Layer the provolone onto the soppressata. Then come the peppers: Just tear the peppers into pieces as you go, nice and casual, scattering them evenly over the cheese.

Give everything a few good lashes of olive oil and cover with the second piece of bread. Slice the sandwich in half on the diagonal.

THE MEATBALL HERO

Where I grew up, meatballs—homemade, of course—were a measure of one's mother. Your mama's meatballs were an unrivaled source of street cred. And everyone thought their mom's meatballs were the best. You defended your mother's meatballs—your mother's honor—to the last. As kids, we loved meatballs so much in part because they were special. You didn't get to eat them every day; they were a Sunday kind of food. Even when you got out of your house, and you could maybe get meatballs at a deli or a slice joint, they seemed still just slightly out of reach. And the meatball hero was the holy grail of sandwiches. It was expensive, it was hot, it was sloppy—man, it was good. You relished every bite.

So there was no way I'd ever open a sandwich shop without including

a meatball hero. But, obviously, I thought carefully about what made the sandwich worthy of such nostalgia, about how to live up to that holy grail hero. Again, it comes down to great ingredients—good bread; freshly ground fatty, humanely raised beef; the best canned tomatoes you can find—but also to getting the meatballs seriously browned and crispy before they hit the sauce. Those crispy browned bits are flavor. There's also a tipping point with the sauce: I want just enough sauce to keep things juicy but not ruin the texture of the bread. You might like the meatballs better just cooked in the sauce, though, so, try it. Cook them both ways and note the difference. You're discovering what you like, figuring out what's best for you.

Once you know how to make these meatballs, you can use them in other ways. You could serve them with a salad alongside, or you could simply cook the meatballs in a heavy skillet and dress them in a lemon, butter, and parsley sauce. You could have them on polenta with an onion gravy. Or you could roll 'em a little smaller and cook them in broth with chile pepper and a little rice—just drop them in, like you would with an Asian soup. Pretty soon, it won't matter if your mama's meatballs were the best in the Bronx, or if you've never been to the Bronx. You'll be making the best meatballs for *you*, and your street cred will be just fine.

Makes 1 sandwich

3 or 4 Meatballs (recipe follows)
½ cup Crushed Tomato Sauce (page 8)
A piece of ciabatta, a hunk of crusty
   bread (if you still have the other
   half of the loaf you used for the
   meatballs, use some of it), or 1 large
   piece Focaccia (page 33), split in half

About 1 tablespoon finely grated
   Parmigiano-Reggiano

Combine the meatballs and tomato sauce in a small saucepan and heat over low heat just until warmed through (you don't want to overcook or toughen the meatballs).

Meanwhile, tear out just a little of the insides of the bottom half of the bread, making a shallow cradle for the meatballs.

Spoon the meatballs, with their sauce, onto the bottom piece of bread. Sprinkle with the Parmigiano. Top with the second piece of bread. Slice the sandwich in half on the diagonal and serve warm.

MEATBALLS

This recipe yields meatballs the size of Ping-Pong balls. I like them this size for a sandwich because they are nice and hefty without being too cumbersome to get your mouth around. But if you are making these for another dish, such as a pasta, or as a snack in their own right, you may want to make them a different size. Determine what size is the most appropriate for your needs.

Makes about 15 large meatballs

½ loaf rustic Italian bread
½ cup whole milk
1 pound ground beef (80/20)
Leaves from ½ bunch flat-leaf parsley,
  chopped (about ¼ cup)
2 to 4 garlic cloves, minced
1 large egg, preferably free-range
½ cup chopped canned tomatoes
2 ounces Parmigiano-Reggiano,
  grated

1 teaspoon dried oregano, preferably
  wild
½ to 1 teaspoon crushed red pepper
  flakes
¾ teaspoon fine sea salt
½ teaspoon freshly ground black
  pepper
1 tablespoon olive oil

Preheat the oven to 350°F.

To start, you want to get as much crust off the bread as you can. Then tear the naked bread into chunks and put them into a bowl (you should have about 2 cups of bread). Pour the milk over the bread and let soak for about 10 minutes, until soft but not falling apart.

Meanwhile, put the meat in a large bowl. Add the parsley, garlic, egg, tomatoes, Parmigiano, oregano (pinching it with your fingers as you add it to release all that heady scent), red pepper flakes, salt, and black pepper and mix with your hands just until everything is combined. Don't overwork the meat, or you'll end up with tough meatballs.

Lift the bread from the milk, squeezing it well so that most of the milk is released back into the bowl. Tear the bread into small pieces, and add it to the beef mixture. Using your hands, bring the whole thing together until everything is just mixed. You want the mixture to hold together so you can form meatballs that keep their shape but are wet enough to stay tender as you cook. Form the mixture into balls a bit larger than a Ping-Pong ball. You should have 15 meatballs.

Grab a skillet that is big enough to hold all the meatballs in a single layer (crowding the pan will bring down the temperature of the oil and the meatballs won't cook quickly enough or get that beautiful sear) and set it over medium-high heat. Add the olive oil and heat until it shimmers. Carefully add the meatballs to the pan (watch for oil splatter). Avoid the temptation to move them around; leaving them alone is the key to getting a beautiful crust on the meat. After about 2 minutes, they should be nicely seared. Flip them and cook on the second side for another 2 minutes or so, until they're nicely browned.

Place the seared meatballs on a baking sheet and pop them into the oven for about 10 minutes, until they're cooked through. Remove the meatballs from the oven. At this point, the meatballs are ready to be served with the sauce of your choice.

Leftover meatballs will keep in an airtight container in the fridge for 3 to 4 days.

PULLED LAMB SANDWICH

Although I grew up an Italian American kid in New York City, I have now spent more than half my life in the Southwest. This landscape—with its people, its traditions, its foods—is my home now. I even managed to get my mother, brother, and father to move out here, and it's where my son and daughter will grow up. One of the reasons I love working with lamb in my kitchens is that it so perfectly interweaves these two threads of my life, my past and my present.

Lamb is a mainstay in Italian cooking (in Italy, everyone eats lamb on Easter), especially in regions like Abruzzo and Molise, much more so than it is in American cuisine. But in the Southwest, lamb has long been a vital part of the culture. In southern Arizona, lambs graze on apples and pears. Just as we are what we eat, so are they. I like to cook lamb with the fruit that sustains the animals and informs the flavor of their meat. It's sort of a play on "what grows together goes together."

I usually braise the lamb using white wine, but I've also cooked it in tea. The tea came about by accident—I was making the dish and realized I didn't have any wine, but I did have some pitchers of iced tea. It was Earl Grey, and I thought that the bergamot flavor might work well with the meat—and it did. I like to do that, to use what I have on hand. Sometimes these accidents work really well. Sometimes not. But the successes outweigh the failures.

Makes 2 sandwiches

About ¼ pound Pulled Lamb (page 92)
About 2 tablespoons gravy from the
    lamb
2 pieces ciabatta, or crusty bread, split
    in half, or 2 large pieces Focaccia
    (page 33), split

A generous handful of salad greens of
    your choice (such as escarole hearts,
    arugula, radicchio, or even cabbage,
    cut into thin, thin strips)
1 tablespoon Cider Vinegar Dressing
    (page 50)

Reheat the lamb in the gravy (or the cooking juices if you didn't make gravy). Pile the lamb onto the bottom halves of the bread. Spoon a tablespoon or two of gravy over the meat.

Quickly toss the greens and dressing together in a bowl. Arrange the greens on top of the lamb. Cover the sandwiches with the top halves of the bread. Slice the sandwiches in half on the diagonal and serve warm.

PULLED LAMB

Serves 4 to 6

One 4-pound bone-in lamb leg or
   shoulder, preferably local
Fine sea salt and freshly ground black
   pepper
3 tablespoons extra virgin olive oil
4 medium white or yellow onions,
   chopped
4 medium carrots, peeled and chopped
4 celery stalks

½ pound mixed seasonal fruits, such
   as apples, pears, and/or plums,
   cored or pitted and cut into large
   dice
15 bay leaves, preferably fresh (see
   Note)
One 750 ml bottle white wine or a
   generous 3 cups brewed Earl Grey tea
3 to 4 quarts chicken stock

An hour or so before you plan to cook, take the lamb out of the refrigerator
and season it with salt and pepper. Let it come to room temperature (this
helps the meat cook more evenly).

Preheat the oven to 325°F.

Once the lamb has reached room temp, set a large Dutch oven over
high heat and add the oil to the pot. When the oil is hot but not smoking,
carefully add the lamb and sear it, turning it as necessary to get a sear on
all sides. When the lamb is golden brown and nice and crispy on all sides,
remove it from the pot and set it aside.

Add the onions, carrots, celery, and fruit to the pot and cook, stirring
every now and then, until the onions have good color and the fruit has
released some of its juices. Scrape everything up from the
bottom of the pot with a wooden spoon, then add the bay leaves
and wine or tea, bring to a boil, and cook until the liquid has
reduced by about half.

Tuck the lamb back into the pot and add enough chicken
stock to come halfway up the sides of the lamb; the stock
shouldn't cover the meat, because you want it to roast and
braise at the same time. Transfer the pot to the oven, cover, and
cook low and slow for about 4 hours, basting the meat every
half hour or so with the braising liquid, until it is falling off the
bone (because you'll be pulling the lamb for sandwiches, you

**Note: This recipe
calls for 15 bay
leaves, which may
seem like a lot,
but I love them—
they are one of the
most underrated
ingredients and there
is something so
ancient about them.**

THE CHURROS JOURNEY

The lamb we use, the Navajo-Churro breed, was brought to the Americas by the Spaniards in the sixteenth century; the Churros were the first breed of domesticated sheep in the New World. Within a century, the Navajos had acquired numerous flocks of Churros through trading, and they had rapidly became an integral part of their economy and culture (many of the earliest, most prized Navajo textiles were woven from Churro wool). By the 1930s, as a result of the Navajos' tremendously successful husbandry, their livestock flocks had grown to just over half a million. Claiming that the flocks were not supportable because of the extreme drought conditions of the Dust Bowl, however, the federal government ordered a forced stock reduction and the vast majority of the Churros were slaughtered. By the 1970s, there were fewer than fifty of the sheep left. Happily, since the '70s, forward-thinking breeders have been working to grow and preserve the breed, and the Navajo-Churro are no longer threatened with extinction, though they're still considered a rare breed. I love that the story of the Churro is a story of survival against all odds, one that's intimately tied to this land and its history. It gives me great pride to be able to use them in our restaurants.

want to make sure it is really broken down). Remove the lamb from the oven and let it cool in its juices for about 15 minutes.

Carefully scoop the lamb out of the pot and set it on a rimmed baking sheet. Use two forks to shred the meat as you pull it from the bone. Let cool, then transfer to a storage container. (The lamb can be refrigerated in the cooking liquid for up to 4 days. When ready to serve, remove it from the liquid and, if you like, make gravy as described below.)

You can make an awesome gravy by straining the braising liquids and solids left in the pot: Remove and discard the celery, then strain the braising liquid through a sieve set over a bowl. Using a wooden spoon, push the solids against the mesh to get all of the delicious concentrated flavor of the fruit juices.

Let the strained liquid sit for half an hour or so, until most of the fat rises to the top, then skim off as much of the fat as you can—don't worry about being too thorough. Pour it into a saucepan and boil to reduce it to the consistency of a sauce.

PASTA & GRAINS

INTENTION & ATTENTION: FIRST IMPRESSIONS

I have spent most of my working life focused on pizza, but pasta is where my relationship with food and cooking began. It's the first thing I can remember eating. Aunt Margie, my great-aunt, lived downstairs from us. She was one of the best cooks I've ever known. When I was a child, I watched her roll out paper-thin sheets of dough for tagliatelle or bring together a Bolognese—intuitively, without measuring spoons or cups. I especially loved seeing her transform ropes of pasta dough into the small ear-shaped pasta called orecchiette, using her thumb to create the little hollows that would capture the gravy—the red sauce—that was like the lifeblood of our dinner table. Every time I sat down to a bowl of Aunt Margie's cavatelli or orecchiette, I wondered at how she had transformed just flour and water into *food*. Watching her taught me to engage deeply with the process of making food, to bring my intention and my attention to the work table, to the stove, to the table. And so those twin habits so central to cooking, intention and attention, were imprinted in me early on in the family kitchen.

I knew that Arizona was—and is—home to a number of heritage wheat strains; in fact, the state exports a lot of durum wheat to Italy for pasta making. I was using that beautiful flour for my pizzas, and I loved the backward logic of it: This strange place that had become my home was sending back to my ancestral home, the place that had so profoundly shaped my palate, an ingredient crucial to the food at the heart of the Italian identity. So when we opened the second location of my pizzeria, and I realized there was the possibility of adding a few pastas to the menu, it felt natural. I felt as though my cooking life had come full circle, back to Aunt Margie's kitchen.

With pasta, cooking with intention is the first step. Not only do you need to choose the particular pasta shape out of the available array that will best support your sauce, but you also need to decide whether to use fresh or dried pasta for that sauce. This chapter celebrates those choices and the decision-making involved.

Every recipe that follows is an opportunity to put things in balance, to consider what makes good things good, and to think about where any new inspirations might lie. Once again, I hope to arm you with the thread that connects every chapter in this book, that what makes a great salad is at heart what makes a great pizza and that what makes a great pizza is what makes a great pasta: the opportunity to use optimal ingredients that you honor with intention and attention.

SPAGHETTI WITH CRUSHED TOMATO AND BASIL

This one is more ritual than recipe and, for me, a most perfect alchemy, arming the most novice of cooks with a precise and measured objective. I love fresh pasta, but, I must admit, I equally love a dried pasta that is select heritage grain, preferably organic, skillfully milled and extruded under the immense pressure of antique brass dies, and dried in a time-honored tradition. The same goes for tomatoes. Whether it's a rumor or a tomato, consider the source—as well as how and where it was grown and whether it was picked at the height of ripeness. Both pasta and tomatoes have a permanent place in my pantry.

Serves 4

2 tablespoons extra virgin olive oil
2 garlic cloves, smashed and peeled
1 pound dried spaghetti (the best you can find)
One 28-ounce can whole tomatoes (the tastiest available)
Fine sea salt and freshly ground black pepper
2 to 4 fresh basil leaves

A handful of finely grated Parmigiano-Reggiano

Bring a large pot of well-salted water to a boil over high heat.

Meanwhile, just before the water comes to a boil, warm the olive oil in a nice big saucepan over medium heat until it is hot but not smoking. Add the garlic cloves and tilt and tip the pan so the garlic is immersed in the oil. Using a good amount of oil instead of a surface film of oil means both that the oil is less likely to

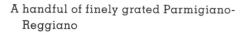

scorch and that you are almost poaching the garlic; flattening the garlic gives it more surface area, which helps it color evenly and better infuse the oil with its flavor. Cook until the garlic is golden, about 1 minute.

Add the spaghetti to the vigorously boiling water and give it a stir. Now you've got about 9 minutes to finish the dish. Add the tomatoes to the pan of oil and garlic and use a wooden spoon to give the tomatoes a good crushing— really get them into that infused oil. Season them with a little salt and pepper and let cook down for 7 to 8 minutes or so, using the spoon to break the tomatoes up further.

The last minute of cooking time for the spaghetti is going to be in the pan of sauce. Drain the spaghetti and add it to the sauce. Add the basil and let everything simmer for a minute or so, until the spaghetti is perfectly al dente. Taste it and see.

Immediately remove the pan from the heat and toss the pasta in the sauce until coated. Add the Parmigiano, stir, and serve immediately.

TAGLIATELLE WITH LEMON

This is another dish of utmost simplicity, but where Spaghetti with Crushed Tomato and Basil (page 98) is a celebration of the pantry, of foods preserved at the optimal moment, this one hinges entirely on the moment of present-freshness; tagliatelle with lemon is about the fleeting now. It is a dish to make when lemons hang heavy, perfumed, and bright, and you can, if you're lucky, pluck a couple from a backyard tree. The recipe is about taking advantage of the opportunity that citrus season presents, to use the sweet-and-sour acidic gift of lemons.

Serves 4

½ cup fresh lemon juice
½ cup plus 2 tablespoons extra virgin olive oil
½ cup finely grated Parmigiano-Reggiano
Fine sea salt and freshly ground black pepper
6 garlic cloves, smashed and peeled

6 bay leaves, preferably fresh
3 ounces fresh spinach
Pasta Dough 1 (page 118), cut into tagliatelle, or 1 pound fresh tagliatelle
4 tablespoons unsalted butter, cut into 4 pieces, at room temperature

Bring a large pot of well-salted water to boil over high heat.

Meanwhile, combine the lemon juice, ½ cup of the olive oil, and the Parmigiano in a bowl and whisk until completely emulsified and thickened. Season with salt and pepper. Set aside.

Heat the remaining 2 tablespoons olive oil in a large saucepan over medium heat. Add the garlic and toast it in the oil until it's golden, about 1 minute. Add the bay leaves and let them infuse the oil for a minute, then add the spinach and sautée until wilted, about 1 minute. Add the lemon juice mixture, increase the heat to high, and bring to a boil.

Meanwhile, drop the tagliatelle into the vigorously boiling water and give it a stir. Cook until tender yet still firm, about 5 minutes.

Drain the pasta and add to the lemon sauce. Reduce the heat and simmer for a minute or so, until the sauce has cooked down somewhat and clings to the pasta. Remove the pan from the heat, add the butter, and toss well. Serve immediately.

Tagliatelle with
Lemon and Polpette
di Ceci (page 172)

PASTA E FAGIOLI

Pasta e fagioli, essentially a bean stew thickened by the pasta that is typically cooked directly in it, is a deeply homey dish—it's a peasant dish, one that can sustain you through a long winter or a hard day's work. Its humble ingredients and origins, however, do little to convey its deliciousness. It is eaten all over Italy, and there are as many variations as there are cities and towns—make that households. Some folks like it more brothy; others like it creamier, with half the cooked beans mashed for body. Some cook the pasta separately to ensure that it remains al dente and add it to the beans at the table. I like to keep it simple, with the focus on the beans.

Pasta e fagioli offers a great opportunity for exploring heirloom beans. I like to use tepary or white emergo beans and chickpeas, which are grown here in the Southwest, though you can make this with other good dried beans, as suggested below. The Tohono O'odham people have grown teparies in Arizona since ancient times—they're one of the most drought- and heat-tolerant crops in the world. I love white tepary beans for their sweetness and brown teparies for their nuttiness—and both types for the fact that they don't break down in soups, even as their centers go creamy. White emergo beans are bigger than lima beans, meaty

and really delicious, with a silky texture. Just as with the Churro lamb in the Pulled Lamb Sandwich (page 90) and the I'itoi onions in the Crispy Gnocchi with Spring Onions and Goat Cheese Crema (page 113), it gives me a lot of joy to celebrate ingredients that are so deeply tied to the history and land of this spot on earth and to marry them with the culture of my own family's history.

Serves 4

1¼ cups dried emergo beans, white tepary beans, navy beans, borlotti (cranberry) beans, or cannellini beans
2 white or yellow onions, halved
1 whole head garlic, halved horizontally
4 bay leaves, preferably fresh
Fine sea salt
Orecchiette (page 120) or 1 pound dried orecchiette or other sturdy small pasta, such as tubetti or conchiglie

4 tablespoons unsalted butter, cut into 4 pieces, at room temperature
¾ cup finely grated Parmigiano-Reggiano
1 teaspoon dried oregano, preferably wild
Freshly ground black pepper
½ cup fresh flat-leaf parsley leaves, torn
About 2 tablespoons extra virgin olive oil

Soak the beans overnight, or for at least 8 hours, in cold water to cover. Drain and rinse.

Combine the beans, onions, garlic, and bay leaves in a large heavy pot and add enough fresh cold water to cover by 3 inches. Bring to a boil over high heat, partially cover the pot, and reduce the heat to maintain a steady gentle simmer. The beans will take roughly 1 to 1½ hours to cook. Check them after an hour and see how they're doing; once they are starting to get creamy, add 1 to 2 teaspoons salt, to taste (adding salt at the start of the cooking can prevent the beans from getting soft).

When the beans are cooked to your liking, stir in the orecchiette. There should be enough water in the pot to just cover the beans and pasta; if not, add more as necessary. Increase the heat to high, bring the beans back to a boil, uncovered, and cook until the pasta is al dente (the time will vary depending on whether you're using fresh or dried pasta).

Remove the pot from the heat as soon as the pasta is al dente, add the butter and Parmigiano, and give everything a good stir. Add the oregano, pinching it between your fingers to release its fragrance, and stir again. Taste for seasoning and add salt if needed and pepper to taste.

Divide the pasta e fagioli among four bowls and finish each bowl with some of the torn parsley and a generous drizzle of olive oil.

SUNDAY GRAVY

Sunday gravy—just the words make me smile. They take me home, back to the place I came from, to the hard wooden pews of our family church and the seemingly eternal Sunday mass, and the glorious meal just on the other side of that long, long service. On those mornings, we all rose early. As we ate our cereal, my brother and I would watch our mom put on a giant pot for the gravy, adding sausages, meatballs, beef chuck, chicken thighs, pork bones, pork neck, whatever was on hand to the pot. Once we were at church, it was the thought of those aromas and flavors, of that meat burbling away in its big bath of winey tomato sauce, that got us through. I knew that not too long after we got home, we'd be gathering around the table, not just me and my mom and pop and brother, but also Aunt Margie and Uncle Red and my grandparents. It was as if the Sunday gravy itself brought us together, as if it were another member of our family. All across the country, families just like ours were doing the same thing. A sacred dish for a sacred day.

Sunday gravy isn't so much a formal recipe as it is an improvisation, a braise of meat in rich wine-infused tomato sauce that you adjust depending on what's in the fridge and how many mouths you need to feed. You always want to include some sausages. Some short ribs would be great. Pork chops or pork shoulder. Bones or no bones. It's up to you. I sometimes use chicken legs, thighs, or wings. You could even include a batch of meatballs or some braciole. And if you buy Parmesan by the chunk or by the wheel, you probably have some rinds on hand—throw a couple of them into the pot. They will give the Sunday gravy a mysterious, ancient, warm, deep flavor. It's all about volume and balance. Every family has its own version, and even that can change from week to week. There is no wrong recipe.

I think most cultures have a dish like this—dishes that are cooked long and slow, that don't require much attention. They give us time to talk and prepare for the meal. The kids can run around, the adults can have a glass of wine. All the while, the Sunday gravy is just simmering away, waiting for us. And in its aroma, our struggles, our joys, our memories, our family stories, our rituals, our traditions, our love are both captured and dispersed.

Serves 6 to 8

¼ cup olive oil

About 4½ pounds meat—such as a mix of sausages, chuck roast, short ribs, pork chops, and/or pork shoulder roast (see headnote)

1 white or yellow onion, halved

4 garlic cloves, smashed and peeled

6 bay leaves, preferably fresh

2 cups red wine

4 cups Crushed Tomato Sauce (page 8), or as needed

A couple of Parmigiano-Reggiano rinds (optional)

Cavatelli (page 121) or 1 pound dried cavatelli

Extra virgin olive oil

Fine sea salt and freshly ground black pepper

Grab a nice big Dutch oven or other heavy pot: The first step in a killer Sunday gravy is browning your meat. So, set that pot over medium-high heat and add some of the olive oil (divide the oil accordingly, depending on how many batches you are cooking). When the oil is hot but not smoking, working in batches, add the meat and let it get a really good sear, about 2 minutes per side; transfer the meat to a large platter as it is browned. Try not to move the meat around much as you sear it—this will help it get a beautiful color and crust.

Once all the meat is seared, add the onion and garlic to the pot and use a wooden spoon to get them good and coated in the oil and fat from the meat. Add the bay leaves and stir for a minute or two so they infuse the oil with their herbaceous goodness. Pour in the wine and use the wooden spoon to scrape up the sticky bits from the bottom of the pot, then return the meat to the pot. Let the wine bubble and burble until it's reduced by about half.

While the wine is bubbling down, run the tomato sauce through a food mill or use a blender—you want a silky, velvety texture here.

Once the wine has reduced, add the tomato sauce to the pot. Is the sauce covering the meat? It should be. If it's not, add more sauce. Add the Parm rinds, if you have them, and give everything a good stir. Cover the pot, reduce the heat to a simmer, and cook until the meat is tender and falling apart and the sauce is thickened and looking like it will cling lovingly to pasta, 1 to 2 hours (the timing will depend on what meats you are using).

Meanwhile, when the gravy is closing in on ready, bring a large pot of well-salted water to a boil over high heat.

Add the cavatelli to the vigorously boiling water and cook until it is just shy of al dente (timing will depend on whether you are using fresh or dried pasta). Drain, toss with a little extra virgin olive oil, and set aside.

When the gravy is good to go, you have two choices: Take the meats out of the sauce and serve them on the side, or take the meat off the bones and toss it all back into the gravy. Either way, add the cavatelli to the sauce, toss well, and cook for a minute or so to finish it.

Add some salt and pepper to the sauce, taste, and adjust the seasoning as necessary.

Set the pot on the table (and the platter of meat if that's how you are serving it). Gather your crew. Relax. Pass the Sunday gravy.

PAPPARDELLE BOLOGNESE

I love making food I have a reference for—I love thinking back on the various iterations of a particular dish I've eaten at different times in my life and mulling over what made them stand out. Looking back on my life, I find that it's only been a study of what makes good things good. That's one of the reasons I like making Bolognese so much—it is a classic that rewards thoughtfulness and patience; but it is also flexible and forgiving. Every time I make Bolognese, I get to play with all of the opportunities it offers to determine what makes a good version good.

The first thing I look at is the meat. I prefer to use humanely raised, grass-fed beef. We use 80/20 beef, with 20 percent fat, and the long, slow cooking process helps to render the fat, resulting in a creamier ragù. The next question is how fine to grind the beef. At our restaurants, we actually grind the beef and vegetables together. The meat stays juicier, lighter, and moister this way, and grinding them together helps achieve the texture I like: The sauce is smoother, with no obtrusive chunks of carrots or onion or celery. At home, you're not as likely to have a meat grinder, so it makes sense to buy ground beef from your butcher. You could achieve a similar effect by bumping the veggies in a food processor. But you know what? You might prefer a less harmonious profile. You might want a chunkier sauce with discrete pieces of veg—and that's all good too. But do chop the veggies into a consistent size, so everything plays well together and browns evenly.

The real key here is time, which brings forward the deepest flavors from all the ingredients and then marries them. The result is a luscious, full-bodied sauce, perfect for a good wide noodle like pappardelle. So, pour yourself a glass of wine (you may even want to splash a little into the pan—another opportunity to deepen and layer the flavors), grab your trusted old wooden spoon, and settle in.

Serves 4

5 tablespoons extra virgin olive oil

3 tablespoons unsalted butter

½ pound ground beef (80/20)

1 medium carrot, peeled and finely chopped

1 medium white or yellow onion, finely chopped

1 celery stalk, finely chopped
1 garlic clove, sliced
2 bay leaves, preferably fresh
¼ cup red wine (optional)
¾ cup Crushed Tomato Sauce (page 8)
Fine sea salt and freshly ground black
  pepper
Pasta Dough 1 (page 118), cut into
  pappardelle, or 1 pound fresh
  pappardelle

2 tablespoons unsalted butter and/or a
  handful of finely grated Parmigiano-
  Reggiano (optional)
Finely grated Parmigiano-Reggiano,
  for serving

Warm the olive oil and butter in a large heavy saucepan over medium heat until the butter has melted and is just beginning to foam. Add the ground beef and brown it really well, separating any clumps with a wooden spoon so it cooks evenly. Once you've got good color and good crust on the meat, add the chopped vegetables, garlic, and bay leaves, stirring to scrape up any browned bits, and cook until the vegetables are soft, the onion is translucent, and all the vegetables are golden, 10 to 15 minutes.

Add the wine, if using, and stir to deglaze the pan. Once the wine cooks off, add the tomato sauce, stir well, and bring to a simmer. Then reduce the heat to medium-low and cook the sauce gently until it has thickened and a thin layer of fat is visible, 1 to 1¼ hours. Taste and season with salt and pepper as needed.

Meanwhile, about 20 minutes before the sauce is done, bring a large pot of well-salted water to a boil over high heat.

Add the pappardelle to the vigorously boiling water and cook until it is just shy of al dente, about 6 minutes. Drain, reserving a cup or so of the pasta water.

Add the pasta to the sauce and toss over medium-high heat for another minute, adding a little of the reserved pasta water to loosen the sauce if needed. You can finish with the butter for extra depth and/or a little Parm if you like.

Toss well and divide among four plates. Serve immediately, with grated Parmigiano on the side. Whoever finds the bay leaves has to cook the next dinner!

LASAGNA AL FORNO

Note: At our restaurants, we use our rich basic pasta dough for this, rolling it out so thin we don't even need to cook the lasagna noodles before assembling the dish. But in the interest of practicality and ease for home cooks, here we give instructions for using store-bought "oven-ready" noodles, available in most supermarkets.

In Italian American cooking, lasagna without ricotta is practically a sacrilege. And in Italy, lasagna layered with ricotta isn't uncommon. But in Naples, where the first formal recipes for lasagna appeared, the pasta sheets were layered more simply, with just ragù, *besciamella* (béchamel), and grated Parmigiano-Reggiano. I've riffed on that Neapolitan style here but taken it a notch further toward minimalism—this guy is meatless. This is a dish I'd serve, along with a beautiful big green salad, if friends were coming over for dinner and a low-key night of wine and conversation around the table.

Serves 8

FOR THE BESCIAMELLA

2 tablespoons unsalted butter
3 tablespoons plus 1 teaspoon all-purpose flour
3 cups whole milk
2 bay leaves, preferably fresh
1 white or yellow onion, halved
1 teaspoon fine sea salt
¼ teaspoon freshly grated nutmeg

FOR ASSEMBLING THE LASAGNA

3¾ cups Crushed Tomato Sauce (page 8)
12 oven-ready lasagna noodles (from an 8-ounce package)
Fine sea salt and freshly ground black pepper
¼ cup extra virgin olive oil
2 cups finely grated Parmigiano-Reggiano
12 fresh basil leaves

Preheat the oven to 350°F.

To make the besciamella: Melt the butter in a medium saucepan over medium-low heat. Add the flour, whisking as you go, and continue to whisk until completely smooth. Increase the heat to medium-high and cook the mixture (roux) until it turns a light golden color, 5 to 7 minutes, whisking occasionally to prevent scorching.

Meanwhile, combine the milk, bay leaves, and onion in a medium saucepan and heat, stirring occasionally, over high heat until the milk is just shy of boiling, about 10 minutes. Remove from the heat, remove the onion and bay leaves, and discard.

Slowly pour the hot milk into the roux, whisking constantly, and increase the heat to high, bringing the mixture to a boil. Reduce the heat to medium-low and simmer, whisking constantly, until the sauce is the consistency of a thick gravy, 8 to 10 minutes. Remove from the heat, add the salt and nutmeg, and stir.

To assemble the lasagna: Ladle ¾ cup of the tomato sauce over the bottom of a 9 x 13-inch baking dish. Dollop a scant ½ cup of the besciamella evenly over the tomato sauce. Top with 3 of the lasagna noodles, covering the sauces completely. Sprinkle with salt and pepper and drizzle with 1 tablespoon of the olive oil. Dollop another ½ cup of the besciamella over the noodles and spoon another ¾ cup of the remaining tomato sauce over the besciamella, filling in all the bare spots. Sprinkle ½ cup of the Parmigiano over the sauces and top with 3 of the basil leaves. Top with 3 more lasagna noodles, and continue the layering so that you have a total of 4 layers of noodles, with a final layer of the remaining Parmigiano and basil leaves.

Cover the baking dish loosely with foil and bake for 45 minutes. Uncover the lasagna and bake for about 20 minutes longer, until the top layer is crusty around the edges. Remove the lasagna from the oven and let it rest for 30 minutes before serving.

Note: Make the besciamella ahead of time and let rest, covered, for about an hour.

Note: You can bake the lasagna ahead and let it stand, covered, at room temperature for up to 3 hours. To rewarm it, cover it loosely with foil and place in a preheated 325°F oven for about 15 minutes, or until heated through.

CRISPY GNOCCHI WITH SPRING ONIONS AND GOAT CHEESE CREMA

Just as I like to think of fresh mozzarella as a "harnessed" glass of milk, I like to think of gnocchi as a harnessed potato. The goal with gnocchi is to use just enough binding ingredients to retain the integrity of the potato, so that its flavor shines and you end up with delicate, not floury, dumplings. I bake the potatoes rather than boil them, as this concentrates their goodness; and because they don't take on any extra water, you end up with a really fluffy texture that needs a minimum of other ingredients to bring it to a happy place. I like nice big russets for gnocchi, but Yukon Golds work well too. When it comes to ricing the potatoes and forming the dumplings, taking a more passive approach leads to the most tender results—like a lot in life. Handle the potatoes minimally and with the least amount of agitation. If you happen to have a gnocchi board (sometimes called a cavatelli board, see page 121), you will, of course, want to use that to form the gnocchi, but a fork works fine.

A great thing about gnocchi is that you can make them well ahead of time: Cook them, then chill them down and just reintroduce them to boiling water to reheat. Or reheat them in a pan with some hot oil and butter, as in this recipe, and then, when they're turning crisp and beginning to color, add some more butter and sage. They'd also be great tossed with some Sunday Gravy (page 105); in that case, just reheat them in boiling water before tossing them with the sauce.

Here the gnocchi are paired with a luscious charred spring onion and goat cheese crema. The sauce was inspired both by my childhood love of onion dip (which, I should admit, has never really gone away) and, more important, by my friend Gary Nabhan, an ecologist, ethnobotanist, and writer who has dedicated much of his life to preserving Southwestern agricultural plants and who introduced me to the I'itoi onion.

The Spaniards brought I'itoi onions to the Americas in 1699, but it was the Tohono O'odham people who gave them a home in the Sonoran Desert and named them for a sacred mountain where they grew. For almost three hundred years, I'itois thrived in southern Arizona, but by the late twentieth

century, they had become an endangered plant. In the early 1980s, Gary Nabhan and his colleague Mahina Drees began working with the Tohono O'odham Nation to establish gardens for sustainable foods. The Tohono O'odham elders told Gary and Mahina that what they really wanted to do was find seeds for the foods that their grandparents had grown. Out of that conversation emerged Native Seeds/SEARCH, a nonprofit that Gary cofounded to preserve crop diversity in the Southwest. And, thanks to the efforts of the Tohono O'odham, Native Seeds/SEARCH, and Gary, we lucky Arizonans (and anyone with a green thumb) have the I'itoi. The small purple bulbs have a sweet, clean taste like that of shallots and the greens are mildly peppery. For those of you who are not in the Southwest, young spring onions or scallions are a good substitute.

Serves 4

FOR THE GNOCCHI

1 pound russet or Yukon Gold potatoes
1 cup all-purpose flour
1 extra-large egg, preferably free-range, beaten

A pinch of fine sea salt
6 tablespoons extra virgin olive oil

FOR THE CREMA

2 tablespoons extra virgin olive oil
16 I'itoi or spring onions or scallions, trimmed
2 tablespoons unsalted butter
Fine sea salt
4 garlic cloves, smashed and peeled

¼ pound fresh goat cheese, crumbled
¾ cup crème fraîche
2 cups vegetable stock
¼ cup finely grated Parmigiano-Reggiano
Freshly ground black pepper

Preheat the oven to 350°F.

To make the gnocchi: Puncture each potato a couple of times with a fork. Bake directly on an oven rack for 45 minutes, or until tender when pierced with a sharp knife.

While the potatoes are still warm, peel them and pass them through a food mill or potato ricer onto a clean work surface, forming a mound.

Sprinkle the flour over the mound of potatoes, then make a well in the center of the mound. Add the beaten egg and salt to the well and, using a fork, gradually incorporate the dry ingredients into the egg, just until mixed

together. Lightly flour your hands, bring the dough together, and knead gently until a ball forms, 2 to 3 minutes. The dough is ready when it is no longer sticky or tacky.

Bring a large pot of salted water to a boil. Set up a large ice bath (a bowl filled with equal amounts of ice and water). Lightly flour a large baking sheet.

Meanwhile, pull off a piece of dough the size of a tennis ball and roll it under your palms on a lightly floured work surface into a rope about 1 inch thick. With a sharp knife, cut it into 1-inch pieces. Hold a fork with its tines against the counter and its back toward you, roll each piece of dough down the back of the fork to get the traditional gnocchi grooves, and set each gnocco on the floured baking sheet. Repeat with the remaining dough.

Drop the gnocchi into the boiling water and cook until they float to the surface of the water, about 1 minute. Use a spider or a slotted spoon to transfer the gnocchi to the ice bath. Let sit for a couple of minutes, then drain well. Transfer to a bowl and toss with the olive oil. (The gnocchi can be made ahead and stored, covered, in the refrigerator for up to 2 days.)

To make the crema: Heat a large skillet over medium-high heat. Add the oil and heat until hot, then add the onions and sear them all over. Wrap them in foil and set aside to steam for about 10 minutes.

Add the butter to the pan and heat until it has melted and is very hot. Add the gnocchi, season with salt, and sauté until they are seared on all sides and crisp, about 2 minutes. Remove the gnocchi from the pan and set aside.

Meanwhile, unwrap the onions and roughly chop them.

Add the onions and garlic to the pan and sauté for a minute or so. Take the pan off the heat, add the goat cheese and crème fraîche, and stir until really creamy.

Return the pan to the heat, add the stock, and increase the heat to high. Bring the sauce to a boil, stirring occasionally, and cook until reduced by half. Add the Parmigiano, stir well, taste, and add salt if necessary and pepper to taste.

Add the gnocchi to the sauce and toss to coat and warm through. Serve immediately.

PASTA DOUGH 1

We use this dough for pastas like pappardelle and
tagliatelle. The large number of egg yolks makes it richer
than a classic southern Italian pasta dough, made with
just semolina and water. And I use imported 00 flour
in combination with semolina for a more delicate result.
Italian 00 flour is a very fine flour that is typically used
for pizza dough, as well as some pastas.

Makes 1 pound

16 large egg yolks, preferably
   free-range
2 cups 00 flour, or as needed
⅔ cup semolina

Beat the egg yolks in a medium bowl.

Combine the 00 flour and semolina in a large bowl and stir to mix
well.

Make a well in the center of the dry ingredients and add the egg
yolks. Using your hands, gradually incorporate the dry ingredients
into the egg yolks, mixing until the dough comes together. Because
different kitchens have different humidity levels and flours can absorb
water differently, you may have to adjust the dough slightly as it comes
together: If it feels too wet, add a little more flour; if it's too dry, add a
teaspoon or so of water.

Turn the dough out onto a floured work surface and knead it until
smooth and elastic; this will take 8 to 10 minutes. Cover the dough with
plastic wrap and let it rest for 10 minutes.

To roll out the dough: Cut the dough into 4 pieces and cover 3
of them with a clean kitchen towel. Flatten the remaining piece of
dough into a rectangle and run it through the widest setting of a pasta
machine. Fold the dough into thirds and run it through the machine

again, then repeat the process one more time. Set the rollers to the next setting and run the dough through them. If necessary, lightly dust the pasta with flour to prevent sticking. Continue to run the pasta through the successive settings of the machine until you have rolled the sheet through the next-to-narrowest setting. Lay the pasta sheet on a lightly floured baking sheet or work surface and repeat with the remaining dough.

Let the dough rest, turning the sheets over once or twice, for 10 minutes, or until no longer sticky.

For tagliatelle: One at a time, roll each sheet through the wider pasta cutter. Coil the tagliatelle into little nests and set on a lightly floured baking sheet or work surface until ready to cook.

For pappardelle: Cut each sheet into 11-inch lengths, then cut lengthwise into thirds, making wide strips.

PASTA DOUGH 2

The doughs for orecchiette and cavatelli are almost the same; the only difference is the proportion of semolina to 00 flour. Both are hearty, toothsome pastas from Puglia. My father was from Puglia, and I grew up eating and making these pastas regularly—they're very much a part of my family food chain.

ORECCHIETTE

Makes 1 pound

1½ cups semolina
1 cup 00 flour, or as needed
1 cup tepid water
Durum wheat or semolina flour for
   dusting

Combine the semolina and 00 flour in a large bowl and stir to mix well. Make a well in the center of the dry ingredients and add the tepid water to the well. Using your hands, gradually incorporate the dry ingredients into the water, mixing until the dough comes together. Because different kitchens have different humidity levels and flours can absorb water differently, you may have to adjust the dough slightly as it comes together. If it feels too wet, add a little more flour; if it's too dry, add a little more water.

Turn the dough out onto a floured work surface and knead it until smooth and elastic; this will take 8 to 10 minutes. Cover the dough with plastic wrap and let it rest for 10 minutes.

Dust a baking sheet with durum wheat or semolina. Form the dough into a ball and cut it into quarters with your trusty dough scraper or a knife.

Note: The orecchiette can be frozen for up to 2 weeks. Freeze on the baking sheet until frozen solid, then transfer to a sealed freezer container.

Working with one quarter at a time (cover the remaining dough with an inverted bowl or a damp towel to keep it from drying out), on a lightly floured surface, roll the dough under your palms into a rope about ½ inch in diameter. With a knife, cut the rope crosswise into ½-inch pieces. Press the center of each piece with your thumb to form it into a saucer-shaped disk. Place the orecchiette on the baking sheet.

Cover the orecchiette with a clean kitchen towel and set aside until ready to use, or for up to 24 hours.

CAVATELLI

Cavatelli is a small ridged pasta made from a slightly denser, firmer dough than that used for most other pasta shapes. It's great to work with because it's almost bulletproof. For example, if you're cooking thin strands of capellini, there's only a tiny window where it is at al dente perfection. But with the heft of cavatelli, the pressure is off.

Note that you will need a cavatelli board—a small ridged board designed for shaping this pasta; you can find one at specialty markets and online. The board can also be used for gnocchi (see page 113), and, in fact, is sometimes referred to as a gnocchi board.

Makes 1 pound

Special Equipment:
Cavatelli board

2 cups semolina
½ cup 00 flour, or as needed
1 cup tepid water
Durum wheat or semolina flour for dusting

Combine the semolina and 00 flour in a large bowl and stir to mix well. Make a well in the center of the dry ingredients and add the tepid water to the well. Using your hands, gradually incorporate the dry ingredients into

the water, mixing until the dough comes together. Because different kitchens have different humidity levels and flours can absorb water differently, you may have to adjust slightly as the dough comes together: If it feels too wet, add a little more flour; if it's too dry, add a little more water.

Turn the dough out onto a floured work surface and knead it until smooth and elastic; this will take 8 to 10 minutes. Cover the dough with plastic wrap and let it rest for 10 minutes.

Dust a baking sheet with durum wheat or semolina. Form the dough into a ball and cut it into quarters with your trusty dough scraper or a knife. Working with one quarter at a time (cover the remaining dough with an inverted bowl or a damp towel to keep it from drying out), on a lightly floured surface, roll the dough under your palms into a rope a little less than ¼ inch in diameter.

With a knife, cut the rope crosswise into pieces just shy of ½ inch. One at a time, place each piece at the top of the cavatelli board (or the back of a fork) and gently press down on it with your thumb to give it the characteristic ridges, then press and push it down the length of the board so it rolls over on itself. You want a little "cave" for the sauce. Place the cavatelli on the baking sheet.

Cover the cavatelli with a clean kitchen towel and set aside until ready to use, or for up to 24 hours.

Note: The cavatelli can be frozen for up to 2 weeks. Freeze on the baking sheet until frozen solid, then transfer to a sealed freezer container.

SPINACH AND RICOTTA CRESPELLE

Many Italian American families celebrate the Feast of the Seven Fishes on Christmas Eve. The day before Christmas was traditionally a fasting day, and the evening meal that served to break the fast was meatless. Instead, it consisted of an abundance of fish dishes—anywhere from seven to thirteen courses. Just one little problem in the Bianco household: My dad is one of the least adventurous eaters in the world. He *hates* fish. So my mom would make these crepes instead. I love the minerality of the spinach and the lushness of the ricotta against the delicate eggy crepes. After they come out of the oven, I let them sit for a bit until they're warm but not hot—actually, I think most food is better just warm or at room temp, when the ingredients have had a chance to marry, to settle, and everything has come together. This is a perfect dish for a dinner party; double the recipe for a larger crowd, if you like.

You can knock the crespelle out in the morning, or even the day before, to lessen the workload. And you can also serve them plain with jam as a treat for the kids.

Aldo Lena, my maternal grandfather.

Serves 4

FOR THE FILLING

1 cup roughly chopped spinach

1 pound whole milk ricotta, drained of excess whey

2 large eggs, preferably free-range

⅓ cup finely grated Parmigiano-Reggiano

1 teaspoon freshly grated nutmeg

1 teaspoon fine sea salt

2 fresh basil leaves, chopped

Freshly ground black pepper

FOR THE CRESPELLE

½ cup whole milk

1 tablespoon unsalted butter, at room temperature

2 large eggs, preferably free-range

¼ cup all-purpose flour

½ teaspoon freshly grated nutmeg

Fine sea salt and freshly ground black pepper

Canola oil

FOR FINISHING THE CRESPELLE

1 tablespoon extra virgin olive oil

2 garlic cloves, smashed and peeled

3 cups Crushed Tomato Sauce (page 8)

2 fresh basil leaves

⅔ cup finely grated Parmigiano-Reggiano

Chopped fresh basil, for garnish

To make the filling: Combine the spinach, ricotta, eggs, Parmigiano, nutmeg, salt, basil, and pepper to taste in a large bowl and mix very well. Set aside.

To make the crespelle: Combine the milk and butter in a small saucepan and heat over low heat, stirring, just until the butter melts. Remove from the heat.

Beat the eggs lightly in a small bowl. Gradually add the milk and butter mixture, stirring to combine.

Put the flour in a small bowl and slowly add the egg mixture, using a fork to incorporate the flour into the liquid. Add the nutmeg and a pinch each of salt and pepper and mix until smooth.

Lightly oil a crepe pan or an 8-inch skillet and heat over medium-high heat until hot. Spoon about 2 tablespoons of the batter into the pan, tilting the pan with a circular motion so that the batter covers the surface evenly. Cook the crepe for about 2 minutes, until the bottom is light brown. Loosen with a spatula, flip, and cook on the other side for about a minute. Transfer to a large plate or a baking sheet. Don't stack the crepes, or they will stick to each other—instead, just slightly overlap them. Cook the remaining crepes, lightly oiling the pan again as necessary.

Preheat the oven to 400°F.

Lay a crepe on a work surface and spoon a generous ¼ cup filling across the bottom third of it. Roll up the crepe like a cigar and set seam side down on a plate. Repeat with the remaining crepes and filling.

To finish the crespelle: Set an ovenproof skillet (large enough to hold all the crespelle) over medium heat. Add the olive oil, and when it is hot but not smoking, add the garlic. As soon as the garlic is golden and aromatic, add the tomato sauce and basil leaves. Increase the heat to high and let everything come together for about a minute, stirring, then remove from the heat.

Add the crespelle seam side down to the pan, nestling them into the sauce. Spoon some of sauce over the tops of the crespelle and sprinkle with the Parmigiano.

Put the pan in the oven and bake the crespelle for about 8 minutes, until the edges are crispy. Remove from the oven and let rest for a few minutes, until the crespelle have cooled a bit but are still warm.

Slide 2 crespelle onto each plate and garnish with chopped basil.

CREAMY POLENTA

Polenta goes back a long way in Italy's history, predating pasta and pizza. It was a staple dish of the armies of ancient Rome—hearty food for soldiers. My mom's family comes from Udine, in Friuli, close to the Alps. She told stories of her grandmother making polenta, pouring it onto a board, letting it set, and then slicing it into pieces with string before topping it with just butter or a stew. At our restaurants, we do serve polenta that we let set and then grill or fry, but more often we serve soft, creamy polenta with butter and cheese stirred into it. You can use anything from Parmigiano-Reggiano to mascarpone, or even a blue cheese like Gorgonzola. Polenta is infinitely adaptable; what really matters is using the best-quality cornmeal you can get, and cooking it long enough for the grain's raw edge to be completely subsumed by the fully developed inherent sweetness.

Serves 4

5 cups water
1 cup polenta (stone-ground yellow cornmeal)
2 teaspoons fine sea salt
½ teaspoon freshly ground black pepper

4 tablespoons unsalted butter, cut into chunks
3 tablespoons finely grated Parmigiano-Reggiano

Bring the water to a boil in a heavy-bottomed medium saucepan over high heat. Slowly pour the polenta into the water, whisking or stirring constantly, then whisk or stir constantly for 2 to 3 minutes, until the polenta begins to thicken. Reduce the heat to medium-low so that the polenta is gently simmering and cook, stirring frequently and adjusting the heat as necessary to maintain a gentle simmer, until the polenta is soft and holds its shape on a spoon, about 1 hour (if the polenta gets too thick before it is cooked, stir in additional water as needed).

Whisk in the salt, pepper, butter, and Parmigiano. Serve immediately.

RISOTTO BIANCO

First things first: I didn't name this dish after myself or the restaurant. *Risotto bianco* simply means "white risotto." The success of this dish relies on the quality of the rice and the attention you bring to its cooking. The classic Italian risotto rice varieties—Arborio, Carnaroli, and Vialone Nano—work fantastically here, but I also love this risotto with brown rice, farro, or some of the heritage short-grain rices found around the world (adjust the cooking time accordingly). Finishing this simple risotto with the best butter and Parmesan you can get takes it from humble to sublime in a nanosecond. The beauty of white risotto is that space it offers, where all things are possible. Once at a tiny trattoria in Istria, on the Adriatic Coast in Croatia, I enjoyed a dish of utmost purity and delicacy: a bowl of silky, savory *risotto bianco* with wild strawberries and finely minced white onion.

Serves 4

8 cups vegetable or chicken stock
2 bay leaves, preferably fresh
6 tablespoons unsalted butter
1 white or yellow onion, finely chopped
2 cups risotto rice (see headnote)

½ cup white wine
Fine sea salt
1 cup finely grated Parmigiano-
    Reggiano
Freshly ground white pepper

Combine the stock and bay leaves in a large saucepan and bring to a boil over medium heat. Lower the heat to keep the stock at a simmer.

Melt 1 tablespoon of the butter in another large saucepan over medium-low heat. Add the onion and cook just until it softens, 1 to 2 minutes. Stir in the rice to coat, then raise the heat to medium and stir for another 2 to 3 minutes. You want to barely toast the rice, without getting any color on it, or your risotto will be slightly brown.

Add the wine and cook, stirring, until it has almost completely evaporated. Add a ladleful of the simmering stock and a good pinch of salt and reduce the heat if you need to so the liquid is only simmering—you want to make sure the rice doesn't cook too quickly, or it won't release the starch that makes risotto creamy. Once the rice has absorbed the stock, add another ladleful and cook and stir until the stock is absorbed. Repeat this process, allowing each addition of stock to be absorbed before adding the next, until the rice is cooked; this will take 15 to 20 minutes. Taste the rice to check: You want some bite but no chalkiness, and the risotto should be creamy. You may not need all the stock; on the other hand, if you run out of stock before the rice is cooked, add some hot water.

Remove the risotto from the heat, add the remaining 5 tablespoons butter and the Parmigiano, and stir until the risotto becomes super creamy. I like my risotto *all'onda*, kind of like a savory porridge; when you shake the pan, it should have a little wave. Season with salt and pepper and serve immediately.

SMALL PLATES

THE WAY WE EAT NOW

In the pizzerias of my youth, pizza was all you would really be there for. Sure, there might have been a chicken Parm on the menu or baked ziti, or a salad of chopped iceberg lettuce, the leaves browning at the tips, overloaded with raw green peppers and raw onions, as well as maybe a little too much oregano and a red wine vinaigrette. But you didn't order that stuff. No way.

And that was OK in the slice joints, where it took only a minute or two to heat up a regular slice and you were good to go. But waiting on a whole pie, that wasn't as great. You were hungry. It would've been nice to have a little something to take the edge off. And I never really forgot that, even when I was working my six-pizza-only menu—in the back of my mind, I was always thinking about sometime in the future, sometime when I'd have a little more room and I could take that opportunity to give people who were expecting less, well, more. A small plate of greens dressed with a vinaigrette made with the highest-quality vinegar. A few slices of prosciutto and a bit of cheese. A little dish of roasted season's-best vegetables, crispy from the heat of the oven.

And, as it turned out, when I had that opportunity, I loved it even more than I'd expected. First, it was gratifying enabling people to eat as they saw fit and put together a meal in the way that made sense for them. The old rules—a main, two sides, all that—don't reflect how we eat now. I loved seeing a couple come in and share a salad, a plate of roasted peppers, some spiedini, and a Rosa pie; or a solo diner sit with a glass of wine, a bowl of spaghetti, and a small dish of wilted greens; or a group of friends sharing three pies and three antipasti and a plate of lamb necks, capping it all off with something sweet. I loved the way people came to our restaurants and made the menu their own,

depending on their moods and needs on any given day. And the smaller plates made that possible, gave people the opportunity to have a bite of this or that, to start or round out their meals with flexibility.

Second, I loved how these smaller dishes, especially the ones I was preparing for our antipasti plates, often gave me the luxury of focusing on just one ingredient. I love to be able to bring everything I have—my attention and intention—to something as simple as, say, a fresh-cut mushroom (a gift the forest gives us) or a carrot from the garden that you just shook the dirt from. It gives me an outlet to be accountable to the bounty we have in this or any part of the world. For this part of the menu especially, I built on things that were at my back door. I wanted people to experience the best our local patch of earth and farmers had to offer, presented with the greatest respect, and I wanted those simple fruits and vegetables and cured meats to be given their due—all of which would translate into a way to begin a meal or to build a meal if you weren't in the mood for pizza or pasta.

Calling these sides sounds almost preliminary, something that can't stand on its own, a filler to distract you while you wait for the main event. Same thing with "side"— calling a dish a side diminishes it somehow. It sounds as if these perfect plates are not good enough to be front and center.

In the end, these smaller plates are all about how you want to eat. If you're eating alone, maybe you want two small dishes instead of one big one. And when there's a whole table of you, these smaller plates really come into their own. Pass them around. Take a forkful or two. They will become part of the conversation, part of the experience. They help define and build your table. And they reflect the way I hope you will use this book: to make and eat food that reflects your needs, your sensibilities— how you eat now.

SPIEDINI

Spiedini are basically anything skewered—and when food's served on a stick, there's a good chance you're having a good time. I love this version in particular. The first time I had it was in northern Italy, in Torino—just a bit of melted cheese with some salty ham. Here we have Fontina doing the business, but it could easily be a tomme or Gruyère—any semi-firm cheese, wrapped up in the prosciutto, with a drizzle of olive oil and a sprinkling of rosemary. Perfect. If you happen to have some sturdy rosemary plants, you can strip the leaves off a couple of the hardier stems, sharpen one end of each one slightly with a paring knife, and use them as your skewers.

Serves 2

One 2-ounce chunk Fontina cheese,
   cut lengthwise into 2 pieces
4 very thin slices prosciutto
Extra virgin olive oil, for drizzling
Leaves from 1 rosemary sprig
A generous handful of arugula
A splash of Red Wine Vinaigrette
   (recipe follows)

Preheat an outdoor grill or the broiler, or set a grill pan over medium-high heat.

   Skewer each piece of cheese lengthwise. Wrap each one in 2 slices of the prosciutto.

   Place the spiedini on a sheet of foil on the grill or under the broiler (2 to 3 inches from the flame), or put them on the grill pan. Drizzle with olive oil, scatter the rosemary leaves on top, and cook, turning once, until the cheese starts to melt and the prosciutto crisps up, a matter of minutes.

Meanwhile, toss the arugula with the vinaigrette in a small bowl until evenly coated. Gently mound the arugula on a plate.

Place the spiedini on the bed of arugula and serve hot.

RED WINE VINAIGRETTE

Makes 1 cup

1½ teaspoons honey
¼ teaspoon dried oregano, preferably wild
¼ cup red wine vinegar

¾ cup olive oil
Fine sea salt and freshly ground black pepper

Set a damp kitchen towel on your counter and place a medium bowl on it, nestling the towel around the bowl to stabilize it. Pour the honey into the bowl and add the oregano. Then slowly add the red wine vinegar, whisking as you do so. Still whisking, slowly drizzle in the olive oil and whisk until the vinaigrette is beautifully emulsified—nice and thick. Add a little sea salt and a few turns of pepper and taste the dressing. Add a little more salt or pepper if you like.

Stored in an airtight container, the dressing will keep for up to 2 weeks in the fridge.

FARINATA WITH SAGE AND ONION

Farinata, a delicate chickpea-flour pancake, is a classic of Genovese cooking, eaten all over Italy. At our restaurants, the dish is really popular with the growing number of gluten-intolerant customers, but originally I didn't put it on the menu with that in mind. Instead of creating "fake" dishes for people with dietary restrictions, I prefer to make food that doesn't rely on substitutions, that is delicious in its own right. Although I have had thicker, more custardy farinata, I prefer my pancakes on the thin and crispy side.

We cook the farinata in the wood-fired oven. The intense heat of the oven floor—around 660°F—is ideal for these. It's easy to work around this at home, though, if you have a pizza stone. (If you don't have a pizza stone, you can do the initial cooking of the farinata on the stovetop over high heat and then finish it in the oven.)

Chickpea flour, also called garbanzo bean flour, is available at some health food stores and online, as well as at Indian markets (where it is called *gram* or *besan*).

Serves 6 (makes three 10-inch farinata)

1 cup chickpea flour (see headnote)
2 cups cold water
About 5 tablespoons extra virgin olive oil
1 tablespoon finely grated Parmigiano-Reggiano

1¼ teaspoons fine sea salt
Freshly ground black pepper
½ large red onion, thinly sliced, or 4 spring onions, thinly sliced
12 fresh sage leaves

One hour before making the farinata, set a pizza stone on a rack in the upper third of the oven and preheat it to its highest setting.

Meanwhile, whisk together the chickpea flour and cold water in a large bowl until smooth. Add 2 tablespoons of the oil, the Parmigiano, salt, and 4 good turns of pepper and whisk to combine. Let stand for at least 30 minutes at room temperature (this helps to fully hydrate the chickpea flour).

When the oven is hot, place a 10-inch ovenproof crepe pan or round griddle pan on the pizza stone and heat for 10 minutes.

Remove the pan from the oven and add a scant tablespoon of olive oil, then add one-third of the onion and 4 sage leaves and return the pan to the oven for about 15 seconds. Working quickly, stir the batter and add one-third of it (about ¼ cup) to the pan. The batter will sizzle and start to set almost immediately. Carefully return the pan to the pizza stone. If using an oven with a built-in broiler, bake the farinata for 12 minutes, then turn the oven setting to broil and cook for 1 to 3 minutes. If using an oven with a separate broiler, bake for 15 minutes, then transfer the pan to the broiler compartment, turn on the broiler, and cook for 1 to 2 minutes. The edges should be golden brown and crisp and the  top flecked with golden spots. Slide the farinata onto a cutting board.

Make 2 more farinata in the same manner with the remaining batter and other ingredients, reheating the pan for 5 minutes and using a scant tablespoon of the remaining oil for each one.

Serve the farinata cut into wedges or strips, or torn apart—whatever you want—and finished with a good grinding of black pepper.

ROASTED FIGS WITH FONTINA AND PROSCIUTTO

Fontina and prosciutto go together so well: fatty, salty, giving. This recipe extends the concept of the Spiedini (page 134) and adds another element—the sweetness of fruit, figs in particular, which are almost honeyed when perfectly ripe. Delicate and difficult to transport, fresh figs are very special (there's a reason there was a fig tree growing in the Garden of Eden). So when you spot these jewels at the farmers' market, go for them—plump, juicy, and sweet.

Let me take this opportunity to give some love to that old classic combination of melon and prosciutto. When melons are in season and as ripe as ripe can be—in Arizona we are blessed with incredible melons—simply combine some rough-hewn chunks of melon and prosciutto on a plate and squeeze a little lemon juice over it all. The acidity of the lemon intensifies the sweetness of the melon and the saltiness of the prosciutto while adding a balancing hit of brightness. It's another object lesson in not standing in the way of great ingredients. Just bring a fork.

Serves 2

6 fresh figs
2 ounces Fontina, cut into 6 cubes or
  chunks
8 thin slices prosciutto
A generous handful of arugula

1 tablespoon Balsamic Dressing
  (page 45)
Fine sea salt and freshly ground black
  pepper
Extra virgin olive oil, for drizzling

Preheat the oven to its highest setting.

Cut a small X in the top of each fig, slicing down through the fruit but being careful not to slice all the way through. Nestle a cube of Fontina into each incision.

Set the stuffed figs, cut side up, in a small roasting pan and roast for 1 to 2 minutes, until the cheese is nice and melted. Remove from the oven.

Arrange the prosciutto slices on two plates, creating a little nest for the arugula. Toss the arugula with the dressing and salt and pepper to taste in a small bowl. Place the arugula in the center of each plate. Nestle the roasted figs into the arugula and finish with a drizzle of olive oil.

GRILLED ZUCCHINI WITH SUNNY-SIDE-UP EGG AND MINT

This dish came about because I really wanted to find a place to put a fried egg on the menu. Fried eggs make me happy. A fried egg, sunny-side up—so you just poke it gently with your fork and that bright sunshine-yellow runny yolk comes oozing out—is pretty satisfying stuff. I like to fry my eggs in butter, but you could use olive oil, or a combination, if you like. The mint and zucchini, a classic pairing, are fresh and bright against the richness of the egg. Depending on the season, though, I might use cauliflower or broccoli, just braised, and instead of mint, fresh flat-leaf parsley or marjoram leaves, or even some crushed dried oregano. And experiment with the cheese too: aged cheddar, Gruyère, and Emmental would all be terrific.

Serves 1

1 tablespoon extra virgin olive oil
2 small zucchini, cut lengthwise into paper-thin slices on a mandoline (get at least 6 slices per zucchini)
Fine sea salt and freshly ground black pepper
1 tablespoon unsalted butter
1 large egg, preferably free-range

1 tablespoon crumbled Parmigiano-Reggiano or mature pecorino
1 tablespoon dried bread crumbs
4 fresh mint leaves
1 tablespoon Charred Onion Vinaigrette (recipe follows), or to taste

Preheat an outdoor grill to high or set a heavy skillet or a grill pan over high heat and get it screamingly hot.

Pour the olive oil onto a small plate and gently drag the zucchini ribbons through it to just coat them, shaking off any excess, then transfer to a large plate. Season the zucchini with salt and pepper. Grill or sear the zucchini ribbons for about 45 seconds on each side—no longer. Set aside.

Melt the butter in a small skillet over medium heat. When the butter begins frothing, crack the egg into the pan and fry sunny-side up, tilting the pan to let the butter lick over the yolk and set the white. I like to let the bottom get a little crispy.

To serve, arrange the zucchini ribbons side by side, slightly overlapping, on a plate and place the egg in the middle. Season the egg with a pinch of salt, then scatter the Parmigiano and bread crumbs on top. Tear the mint roughly and scatter it. Finish by spooning on just enough of the onion vinaigrette to give it all a glossy sheen.

CHARRED ONION VINAIGRETTE

You can use this with so many dishes. Here it brings a savory, velvety finish to the zucchini, with its charred flavor working so well with the egg. You could also use it on a shaved zucchini salad or to finish some fish just off the grill, like sea bass or swordfish.

Makes about 1½ cups

½ large red onion (cut a whole onion crosswise in half)
1 cup plus 1 tablespoon extra virgin olive oil

Juice of 2 lemons (about 6 tablespoons)
Fine sea salt and freshly ground black pepper

Preheat the oven to its highest setting.

Place the onion in a small baking pan. Drizzle with 1 tablespoon of the olive oil and roast for 40 minutes, or until the outer layer is well blackened. Remove the onion from the oven and allow it to cool.

Scrape off the onion's black outer layer and discard. Chop the rest of the onion very fine. Combine the onion, the remaining 1 cup oil, the lemon juice, and salt and pepper to taste in a medium bowl and whisk to blend.

Stored in an airtight container, the vinaigrette will keep in the fridge for up to 1 week.

CHANTERELLES WITH GARLIC AND THYME

Chanterelles are brought to us like gifts by foragers, harvested from their secret hiding places. Their woodsy flavor has both an earthiness and a sense of decadence. Oyster mushrooms, hen-of-the woods mushrooms, and porcini would impart the same spirit and satisfaction.

Serves 2

½ pound chanterelles
¼ cup extra virgin olive oil
2 tablespoons unsalted butter
Fine sea salt and freshly ground black pepper

1 garlic clove, smashed and peeled
½ teaspoon fresh thyme leaves
2 bay leaves, preferably fresh
A splash of fresh lemon juice

Cut the mushrooms into bite-size pieces. Remove any obvious pieces of dirt or debris, but don't wash them, as that can waterlog them.

Heat a large skillet over medium heat and add the olive oil and 1 tablespoon of the butter. When the butter has melted and is beginning to froth, add the mushrooms, season with salt and pepper, and toss quickly to coat. Let the chanterelles sear on one side (don't move them around too much) until they are browned, about 5 minutes, then toss the mushrooms to expose the other side to the heat. The edges should be crispy and the texture firm.

Add the garlic, thyme, and bay leaves and cook until the garlic has softened, 2 to 3 minutes.

To finish, stir in the remaining 1 tablespoon butter and the lemon juice. Season to taste if necessary and serve.

BEETS ROASTED WITH FIG LEAVES

We are blessed to have a fig tree in the garden at our restaurant in downtown Phoenix. I love figs not only because their sweetness never becomes cloying, but also because every time I split one open, it makes me think of a Renaissance painting. Their leaves are also beautiful, and here, fig leaves prevent the roasting beets from scorching while imparting the essence of the fruit itself. It's almost like a magic trick. Think of this as more an inspiration than a recipe. Maybe you're blessed with a lemon tree or an avocado tree. The idea is to add depth of flavor—and to take the taste, aroma, and look of a simple vegetable to the next level.

Serves 4

15 fig leaves (unsprayed)
2 pounds medium beets—a mix of
   golden and red if you like
10 bay leaves, preferably fresh

1½ tablespoons fine sea salt
Freshly ground black pepper, to taste
¼ cup extra virgin olive oil

Preheat the oven to 400°F.

Arrange 7 of the fig leaves on a rimmed baking sheet, covering it entirely. Set the other leaves aside.

Put the beets in a large bowl, add the bay leaves, salt, pepper, and olive oil, and toss to mix. Scoop the contents of the bowl onto the baking sheet and spread the beets out evenly. Cover the pan with foil and roast for 45 minutes, or until the beets are cooked through. To test for doneness, poke the center of a beet with a paring knife or toothpick and lift it up—the beet should slide right off. Remove from the oven and let the beets cool a little, to make them easier to peel.

Once they are cool enough to handle, peel the beets by rubbing them with paper towels; the skin should slide right off.

Arrange the reserved fig leaves on a platter and place the beets on top. Finish with a spoonful or two of the pan juices and serve.

GRILLED RED PEPPERS

Grilling red peppers is almost like alchemy. The fire transforms them, intensifying their sweetness, and charring the skin imparts just a hint of smokiness to the flesh. When you grill-roast red peppers over an open flame, you're really blistering the skin, not cooking the flesh itself. When you remove the skin, you want to leave just a kiss of char. But please don't do this under running water! I like to think I don't yell in the kitchen, but one thing that sets me off is seeing someone washing the skin off peppers and losing all those hard-earned flavors and oils down the drain.

Serves 4

8 red bell peppers
4 garlic cloves, smashed and peeled
5 fresh basil leaves

¼ cup extra virgin olive oil
Fine sea salt and freshly ground black
  pepper

Preheat an outdoor grill to high or heat the broiler; if using a broiler, place an oven rack a few inches below it.

Set the peppers on the hot grill or, if using a broiler, lay them out on a baking sheet and set them on the rack beneath the broiler. Grill or broil the peppers, using tongs to turn them as needed, until the skins char and blacken all over. Transfer the peppers to a bowl, cover with plastic wrap, and let steam and cool.

Once the peppers are cool, peel off the skin (it should come right off) and discard. Halve the peppers and gently remove the cores and seeds.

Put the peppers in a bowl, add the garlic, basil leaves, olive oil, and a sprinkling of salt and pepper, and mix gently. Let marinate at room temperature for at least an hour to marry all the flavors. If you want to marinate the peppers longer, cover the bowl with plastic wrap and refrigerate; they will keep for up to 4 days. Allow them to come to room temperature before serving.

PAN-GRILLED PADRÓN PEPPERS WITH LEMON AIOLI

I love peppers in all shapes and forms, whether hot or sweet or somewhere in the middle—with Padróns, you get all three. Eating them is a fun little gamble: Although most are relatively mild, every so often you'll run into one that brings some serious heat. Blistering the skins adds a depth of flavor and textural contrast, which, paired with the acid hit of lemony aioli and the crunchy coarse sea salt, makes it almost impossible to stop eating them.

Serves 2 to 4

½ pound Padrón peppers
1 tablespoon extra-virgin olive oil
3 tablespoons Lemon Aioli (recipe
 follows)
Coarse sea salt, for sprinkling

Set a large cast-iron or other heavy skillet over high heat and get it good and hot, almost smoking.

Meanwhile, put the peppers in a medium bowl and add the oil, tossing to coat.

When your pan is ready, use tongs to lay the peppers in the pan in a single layer, without touching. (Set the bowl aside.) Cook the peppers, turning them occasionally, until they start to char and blister on all sides, 6 to 8 minutes.

Return the peppers to the bowl, add the aioli and salt, and toss to combine. Serve.

LEMON AIOLI

Makes about 1⅓ cups

2 large egg yolks, preferably from free-range eggs
2 garlic cloves, minced
2 to 3 tablespoons fresh lemon juice

Fine sea salt
1 cup olive oil
1 tablespoon minced fresh flat-leaf parsley

Set a damp kitchen towel on your counter and place a small bowl on it, nestling the towel around the bowl to stabilize it. Add the egg yolks, garlic, 2 tablespoons lemon juice, and a pinch of salt to the bowl and whisk to blend. Whisk in the olive oil, drop by drop at first and then, once the mixture has begun to emulsify, in a thin steady stream, whisking constantly until the aioli is beautifully emulsified—nice and thick. Whisk in the parsley. Taste the aioli and add up to 1 tablespoon more lemon juice, if you like, and salt to taste.

Stored in an airtight container, the aioli will keep for up to 1 week in the refrigerator.

CRISPY ROSEMARY FINGERLINGS

This dish is actually awesome made with any good potato. I like it with fingerlings, but it also works well with russets. Halved fingerlings or wedges of russet potatoes will lead to that blissed-out state of a crispy exterior and an almost meltingly fluffy interior. The potatoes are cooked in two stages: First they are roasted until golden, crispy, and cooked through, and then the Parm is added and they are baked a few minutes longer for a salty, fatty finish. More, please.

Serves 4

1 pound fingerling potatoes, gently
   scrubbed
4 bay leaves, preferably fresh
8 garlic cloves, smashed, in their skins
½ cup extra virgin olive oil
2 tablespoons fresh rosemary leaves,
   roughly chopped

Fine sea salt and freshly ground black
   pepper
1⅓ cups coarsely grated Parmigiano-
   Reggiano
Coarse salt

Preheat the oven to 375°F.

Halve the potatoes lengthwise and put in a large bowl. Add the bay leaves, garlic, olive oil, and rosemary, sprinkle generously with salt and 4 or 5 turns of pepper, and mix well. Lay the potato halves cut side up in a single layer in a baking pan. Pour the oil, herbs, and garlic over the potatoes and roast for 20 to 25 minutes, turning once or twice, until they are crispy and cooked through.

Sprinkle the Parmigiano evenly over the potatoes and bake for about 3 minutes more—you want the cheese to have just a little melt on it. Sprinkle with coarse salt and serve.

ROASTED SWEET POTATOES WITH BAY LEAVES

When I was growing up, sweet potatoes were something I would see only on the holidays. I didn't really like them, probably because they were always candied or cloyingly sweet. Now I love the flavor and texture of a properly cooked sweet potato. Roasting sweet potatoes until they give up their natural sugars and the skin becomes chewy and crispy all at once is one way to enjoy them. Another way is this recipe. Anytime I can find a place for fresh bay leaves, I am happy. I love how bay infuses its herbaceous, heady, almost medicinal flavor into other ingredients. And it's a really nice counterpoint to the sugars in the sweet potatoes.

Serves 4

4 medium sweet potatoes, sliced into
  rounds about ½ inch thick
2 small white or yellow onions,
  quartered

8 bay leaves, preferably fresh
1 cup white wine
Fine sea salt and freshly ground black
  pepper

Preheat the oven to 400°F.

Put the sweet potatoes in a large bowl. Add the onions, bay leaves, wine, and salt and pepper to taste and mix well. Lay the sweet potato slices side by side in a large roasting pan, like a little army of sweet potatoes, overlapping them as necessary to fit. Scatter the bay leaves and onion quarters evenly over them. Pour the wine remaining in the bowl over the potatoes.

Cover the pan with foil and bake for 40 minutes, or until the sweet potatoes have begun caramelizing and turning golden all over. Remove the foil and bake the potatoes uncovered for another 10 minutes or so to crisp.

To serve, arrange the sweet potatoes on plates and pour over any pan juices.

ROASTED ONIONS

Onions are an underappreciated vegetable, one we take for granted, but they are the foundational flavor of so much cooking, and in all their many forms, from raw to caramelized, they can almost instantly transform a dish from bland to balanced. I especially love big sturdy sweet onions sliced thick and roasted slowly. You can use them as a warm ingredient in salads, for a play of temperatures. Or toss them with chopped flat-leaf parsley, and you have a fantastic antipasto.

For me, one of the most important things when using onions is texture. Here charring brings color but allows them to retain an al dente quality, if you'll allow me a pasta reference. We also roast onions for the Wiseguy, but for the pizza topping, we use white or yellow onions.

Serves 4

2 large sweet onions, such as Vidalia, skin left on, sliced crosswise into 4 rounds each

Fine sea salt and freshly ground black pepper

Extra virgin olive oil

Preheat the oven to its highest setting.

Lay the onions out on a rimmed baking sheet. Season with salt and pepper and lash with a generous amount of olive oil.

Roast the onions for 7 minutes and then, using tongs, flip the rounds, and cook for another 7 minutes, or until they are nice and caramelized. Remove from the oven and let cool slightly.

Once the onions are cool enough to handle, remove their skins. They are ready to be used for any preparation you would like.

ROASTED CARROTS

We use these roasted carrots as part of our antipasto plate and we also turn them into a quick warm, savory salad. We mix in a bit of crumbled Stilton, add sherry vinegar, and serve them with the pan juices.

Serves 4 to 6

2 pounds small young carrots, sliced
    into ½-inch-thick rounds
¼ cup extra virgin olive oil

1 garlic clove, chopped
Fine sea salt

Preheat the oven to 400°F.

Put the carrots in a large bowl, add the oil, garlic, and a pinch of salt, and toss together with your hands, making sure that every piece of carrot is coated in oil. Empty the contents of the bowl into a shallow flameproof roasting pan, spreading the carrots out evenly.

Cover the pan with foil and roast for 25 minutes, or until you can pierce the carrots easily with a paring knife. Remove the pan from the oven.

Set the roasting pan over medium-high heat and cook the carrots, stirring occasionally, for another few minutes, until they're golden and almost crispy—I like them with a good bit of color. Adjust the seasoning if necessary and serve.

BRAISED KALE

I love the heartiness and minerality of kale. This cooking method works with all the beautiful variants of kale available now, from regular curly kale to more unusual types like Russian Red. If the kale you get has thick, fibrous stems, remove them from the leaves and blanch them in boiling slightly salted water until tender, 3 to 5 minutes. Then drain the stems, let cool slightly, and squeeze out the excess water. (If you feel like a bit of pasta with your kale, save the blanching water and use it to cook the pasta, giving it additional depth of flavor—think of it as "kale stock.") Roughly chop the stems and proceed with the recipe, adding the stems to the pan with the chopped leaves. If your kale is younger and more tender, simply trim and chop it all and proceed as directed. The braised kale goes beautifully with the Slow-Roasted Lamb Neck (page 178).

Serves 2

3 tablespoons extra virgin olive oil
1 white or yellow onion, thinly sliced
Fine sea salt and freshly ground black
    pepper
5 garlic cloves, thinly sliced

1 teaspoon crushed red pepper flakes
2 large bunches kale, preferably young
    and tender (see headnote), trimmed
    and chopped
1 cup water

Heat the olive oil in a large deep skillet over medium-high heat. When the oil is hot, add the onion and season with salt and pepper. Cook, stirring occasionally, until the onion begins to soften and turn translucent, 3 to 4 minutes. Add the garlic and pepper flakes, stirring to combine, and cook just until the garlic is aromatic and golden, a minute or so.

Add the kale to the pan and season with salt and pepper. Add the water and give everything a good stir. Cover, reduce the heat to medium-low, and cook until the liquid has reduced and the kale is tender, 10 to 15 minutes. Taste and adjust for seasoning. Serve.

ROASTED TOMATOES WITH WILD OREGANO

Slow-roasting tomatoes concentrates their flavor. With the earthy woodsiness of wild oregano, these tomatoes are sweet and intense. We serve them as an antipasto.

Serves 4

8 tomatoes (any variety)
2 tablespoons extra virgin olive oil, plus more for drizzling
Fine sea salt and freshly ground black pepper

A generous pinch of dried oregano, preferably wild
4 garlic cloves

Preheat the oven to 325°F. Line a baking sheet with parchment paper.

If the tomatoes are small, cut them in half; if they're bigger, cut them into quarters. Combine the tomatoes and olive oil in a large bowl, season with salt and pepper, and toss well. Add the oregano, crumbling it with your fingers to activate all that fragrance and flavor. Toss gently.

Arrange the tomatoes in a single layer, skin side down, on the baking sheet. Scatter the garlic cloves around them and add another generous drizzle of olive oil. Roast for 2½ to 3 hours, until the tomatoes have collapsed and are very soft and wrinkled. Remove from the oven and let cool.

The tomatoes can be refrigerated, covered, for up to 4 days. Bring to room temperature before serving.

PAN-ROASTED CAULIFLOWER

Back in the '70s, the only way I encountered cauliflower was boiled to hell and drenched with a butter or cheese sauce. Worse, to me as a kid, raw cauliflower looked kind of like brains. After those early cauliflower traumas, I wasn't in a hurry to give it a second chance. But proper cooking techniques can elevate this seemingly mundane vegetable to the culinary heights it deserves. Cauliflower is insanely delicious when it is roasted so its edges go all crispy and caramelized and it tastes mysteriously rich and complex. I'm keeping it simple and mostly unadorned here, but I love that cauliflower is a great canvas on which you can improvise with all sorts of flavors: I often add a bit of anchovies or raisins or grated lemon zest.

Serves 4

Scant ½ cup extra virgin olive oil
4 garlic cloves, smashed and peeled
4 spring onions or large scallions, trimmed and chopped
1 medium head cauliflower or Romanesco (about 2 pounds), cored and broken into florets

½ teaspoon fine sea salt
Freshly ground black pepper
6 bay leaves, preferably fresh
1 cup white wine
1 lemon
A small handful of fresh flat-leaf parsley leaves, torn

Heat the olive oil in a large skillet over medium-high heat until hot but not smoking. Add the garlic and cook just until it starts to color, a minute or so, then add the spring onions and cook until you can smell the aromatics, another minute or so. Add the cauliflower and season with the salt and pepper to taste. Then let the cauliflower just sit, without stirring, for 5 minutes. You want to get some great, deep color on it, and that's how you do it—no stirring. After 5 minutes, check the underside of a cauliflower piece. Nice and browned? Great. Add the bay leaves, then flip the cauliflower pieces and cook for another 5 minutes, getting good color and caramelization on that side as well.

Increase the heat to high, add the wine to the pan, bring to a boil, and cook until reduced by half. Finish with a squeeze of the lemon.

Scatter the parsley on top and serve.

BIG PLATES & BOWLS

THE BUTCHER, THE BAKER, THE CANDLESTICK MAKER

I always say it takes a village, or a community: Whether butcher, baker, or candlestick maker, we all play a small role in making this world what it is—and this goes straight back to the importance of relationships. With our food, everything is dependent on our relationships—whether with the farmers who raise the crops, or my staff and how I communicate with them about what they're serving—and on everyone who supports the restaurant.

When I was working on this chapter, I started thinking again about why we serve these dishes, why we didn't just stop with pizza and salads, and then sandwiches, and then pasta. What was the opportunity of these dishes? What is the opportunity of "the main dish"? For a lot of people, big plates like these are the main event of the day. They bring people to the table, to break bread together, to communicate. Once again, it's about relationships—not just how food creates and sustains relationships, but also the relationships we have with the food itself, and with those that provide it. Many of these dishes are so at the heart of "family meals"—however you want to define family. And, much more so than the recipes in the other chapters, many

of them feature major animal protein. We live in an era when we can no longer avoid thinking about the realities of eating meat: where it comes from, how it came to our table. So a big plate is an opportunity to be conscious about that specific relationship; as well as an opportunity to forge a relationship with a butcher, or a farmer. Ask your butchers what cuts would be best for the dish you're cooking, and ask them for recipes and ideas. They are part of the community as much as you are. And serving a big plate is also an opportunity to share your love, your own history. When we cook for our friends and families, we become a part of something bigger—a chain of past, present, and future. With every meal I've ever cooked for anyone, I've brought everything, every memory from my past, to the table. So I feel a great responsibility in making this food. I didn't invent it; I inherited it.

ROASTED EGGPLANT WITH TOMATO AND PARMIGIANO-REGGIANO

This is all about best-of-season eggplants: small, sweet varietals without seeds, so they don't need to be salted or leached of bitterness. My favorites are Japanese eggplants, long and slender and the deepest, darkest, almost black purple, which we start seeing here in Arizona in early summer and then through fall. But you could try Chinese eggplants, slightly less sweet, also long and slender, and a bright royal purple; or tiny graffiti eggplant, with their white-streaked skins. Any great eggplant will work, but do taste it raw to see what you're dealing with—how bitter it is, how firm or delicate—so you can accommodate those qualities. Because the eggplant is shallow-fried before you assemble the dish, you not only get that luxuriously yielding fleshy inside, but you also introduce beautiful crispness, color, and char. The tomato here is more of a glaze than a saucy blanket, heightening the sweetness of the eggplant rather than drowning it. The DNA of eggplant Parm is there; it's not so far removed from the familiar, just tweaked. My perfect meal might start with a plate of pasta—say, spaghetti with parsley and bread crumbs—and then a slice of this with a big sturdy salad, a glass of red wine, and some great bread. Maybe a piece of good chocolate and some pomegranate seeds. Beautiful.

If you can't find slender, smaller eggplants, you can use large, firm eggplants, but be sure to taste a piece raw, and if it seems bitter, salt the diced eggplant and let drain in a colander set over a bowl for 20 to 30 minutes. You will see beads of moisture coming to the surface. Rinse off the salt, pat the pieces thoroughly dry, and proceed with the recipe.

Serves 4

1 cup extra virgin olive oil

2 pounds long, slender eggplants, peeled and cut into ½-inch dice

2 garlic cloves, smashed and peeled

½ large white or yellow onion, cut into medium dice

One 14.5-ounce can whole tomatoes

Fine sea salt and freshly ground black pepper

2 fresh basil leaves

6 ounces Parmigiano-Reggiano, coarsely grated

Preheat the oven to 350°F.

Set a large skillet over medium heat and pour in ½ cup of the olive oil. When the oil is warm, after about a minute or so, add half the diced eggplant. (You want to shallow-fry the eggplant in batches, so you don't overcrowd the pan; otherwise, the eggplant will end up steaming or braising, which would result in less flavor and a mushier texture. Of course, if you have two large pans, you can cook both batches at once.) Cook the eggplant, stirring frequently with a wooden spoon, until you get some nice color and crispness, about 7 minutes. Add one of the garlic cloves and cook for another minute, then add half the onion and cook for another 3 minutes or so, until the onion gets some caramelization too.

Add half the tomatoes to the pan and cook, stirring now and then and breaking up the tomatoes with the wooden spoon, until a light sauce forms, about 10 minutes. Season the eggplant mixture with salt and pepper and add one of the basil leaves to the pan. Give everything a quick stir, then transfer to an 8-inch square baking dish and set aside.

Repeat with the remaining ½ cup oil, eggplant, garlic, onion, tomatoes, salt, pepper, and basil. Add to the baking dish and stir to combine.

Pop the dish, uncovered, into the oven and bake for about 10 minutes, until the eggplant is soft but not too soft—you still want some texture there. Scatter the Parmigiano over the eggplant and bake for another 3 to 4 minutes, until the cheese is golden and bubbling.

Remove the dish from the oven and let cool to your preferred temperature. You can eat this hot, at room temperature, or cold.

POLPETTONE

We use the same seasoned ground meat mix for our *polpettone* (meat loaf) as for the meatballs for The Meatball Hero (page 85). You can serve it on its own, or with tomato sauce. Spoon the sauce onto the plates first, so you can get some with each bite. The Potato Salad (page 64) would make a nice side. And, of course, this also makes great sandwiches.

At our restaurants, we wrap the shaped meat loaf in the bacon and then sear it on both sides in a hot pan on the stovetop before baking it. That can be tricky, so for this recipe, we simply cover the loaf with the strips of bacon and do all the cooking in the oven. (Be sure to use thin-sliced bacon.) The results are delicious in either case.

Serves 4 to 6

Meat mixture from Meatballs (page 87)
8 thin slices bacon, preferably
  applewood-smoked

1½ to 2 cups Crushed Tomato Sauce
  (page 8), warmed (optional)

Preheat the oven to 375°F. Line a baking sheet with foil (for easy clean up) and lightly grease the foil.

Put the meat mixture in the center of the baking sheet and shape into a compact loaf about 9 inches long and 4 inches wide. Trim the strips of bacon so they will just cover the top and sides of the meat loaf and arrange the slices crosswise over the meat loaf, overlapping them slightly. Reserve the trimmings for another use.

Bake the meat loaf for 50 to 55 minutes, until an instant-read thermometer inserted in the center registers 155°F. Let rest on the baking sheet for 20 minutes.

Slice the meat loaf and serve warm, with or without the tomato sauce.

PAPPA AL POMODORO

This classic soupy Tuscan dish is all about those amazing tomatoes that come into play in late summer, when they are just on the border of too ripe: When all the tomatoes at the farmers' market are crazy sizes, dented, and splitting, and the farmer is happy to offload them on you, the smart cook sees all their great potential. If you can, get tomatoes with some fragrant stems still attached—they will add a sweet, earthy pungency. It's also about celebrating bread, extending the life of great bread, whether you make it yourself or you live down the street from a great bakery. It's about recognizing that you're actually fortunate to have leftover bread. You could just use stale bread and not bother with the toasting, but I love the extra element that toasting brings—that smoky, charred flavor.

When you put together those tomatoes and the bread, they are transformed into a savory almost-pudding that is humble but celebratory in its power to nurture, and revelatory in its deliciousness—even more so when you finish it all with a lash of fruity olive oil. This is the time to break out that special bottle of oil. It will amp up the lushness of the dish, and the little rivulet of cool oil against the hot soup is a wonderful contrast of temperatures. Then pair this with something a little salty, like some cured meat, a bright green salad, and a big glass of wine.

Serves 4

3 tablespoons extra virgin olive oil, plus more for drizzling
1 white or yellow onion, roughly chopped
4 or 5 garlic cloves, smashed and peeled
4 pounds ripe tomatoes
Fine sea salt

Leaves from a big bunch of basil, torn (reserve a few whole leaves for garnish)
2 bay leaves, preferably fresh
4 slices great rustic bread
A chunk of Parmigiano-Reggiano, for shaving

Set a large pot over medium heat and add the oil. Once the oil is warm, add the onion and cook, stirring occasionally with a wooden spoon, until you get some nice color on it, about 5 minutes. Add the garlic and give everything a quick stir so that the garlic is coated in oil. Then add the tomatoes (just rinsed—no need to dry them, as the residual water clinging to their skins will create beautiful steam to help cook down the sauce), stems and all. Sprinkle the tomatoes with a little salt, then add the torn basil and the bay leaves. Give everything another good stir, so that all the elements are coated with a slick of oil, then stir a few more times so that all the tomatoes have some flecks of onion hugging them. The basil will have wilted and be woven through the other elements, peeking through the redness. Cover the pot with a tight-fitting lid, reduce the heat to low, and let everything simmer and steam for about 10 minutes.

Now lift the lid and check—the tomato skins should have split. Using the wooden spoon, start gently mashing the tomatoes down into a cohesive mass. Once they are all broken down, take the pot off the heat and let cool for about 10 minutes.

Run the tomato mixture through a food mill set over a bowl. The resulting *passata* will be loose and fragrant and smell like summer. Throw it back into the cooking pot.

Toast the slices of bread, then roughly tear them up. Add a few handfuls of bread to the pot and stir to dissolve the bread in the passata, then add more if necessary, until you reach your desired consistency—you want enough bread to thicken the soup but not so much it makes it too thick.

Ladle into bowls, shave a few scrapes of Parmigiano on top of each one, and finish with the reserved basil leaves and a drizzle of olive oil. Really good.

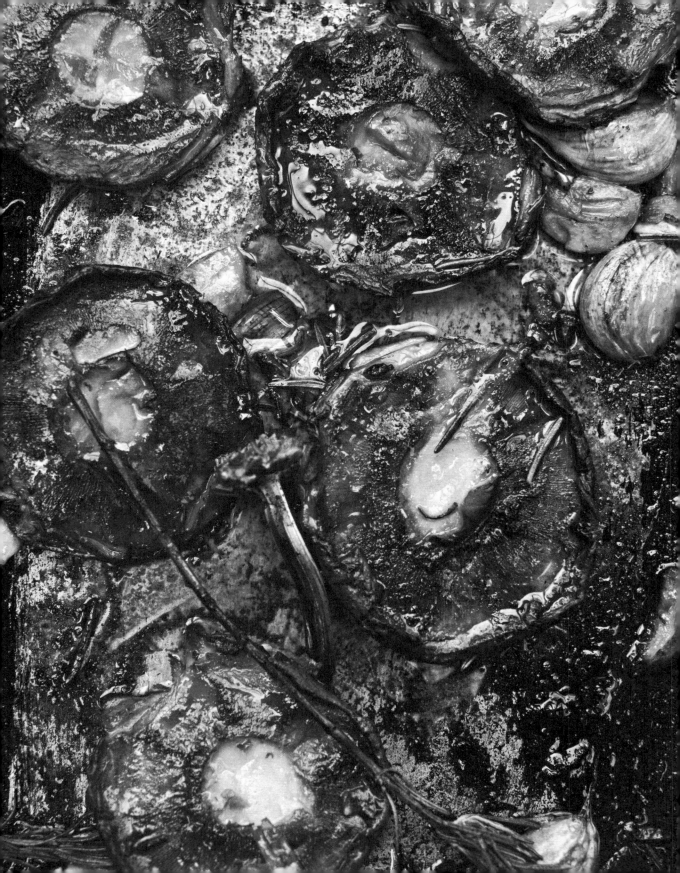

MUSHROOMS AND BEER

Enough said!

I was about fourteen when I started hearing about a very exotic, gourmet item that was receiving heavy advertising rotation on a local radio station. That's right: beer-battered mushrooms. Sure, I had heard about the almost equally exotic beer-battered onion, but wow—this must be something special. White breadcrumbs clinging to pedestrian white mushrooms, deep fried to make sure they were a greasy, crispy, and salty foil to the pint of ranch dressing that accompanied them. But the one thing these manifestations of gastronomy did get right in 1975 is beer and mushrooms, a match made at a corner pub in heaven. This recipe removes the frying of the breadcrumbs and the pedestrian white mushrooms (no disrespect) and brings an earthy, meaty portobello mushroom into play. Darker beers, such as an IPA or classic English porter, provide great flavor and caramelization. Also feel free to experiment with what you have on hand as basically any mushroom and libation will work. As for the herbs, again, use what you have; rosemary, thyme, or tarragon are all good calls. The portobello gives you flexibility as this dish can be served as an antipasto, a vegetarian main dish, or even a sandwich. Also easy is the drink pairing—this dish goes with whatever you have on tap. Cheers.

Serves 4

8 large portobello mushrooms
6 tablespoons extra virgin olive oil
Fine sea salt and freshly ground black
  pepper

8 garlic cloves, smashed and peeled
6 rosemary sprigs
One 12-ounce bottle beer (brown ale,
  pale ale, IPA, stout, or porter)

Preheat the oven to 450°F.

Brush the mushrooms lightly to remove any dirt clinging to them. Gently pinch the stems and pull them off (you can save the stems to use chopped in a stock or compost them). Take a small spoon and gently scrape away the gills from the mushroom caps.

Lay the mushrooms in a large flameproof roasting pan, gill side up. Drizzle with the olive oil and use your hands to get them all good and

coated with oil, then season with salt and pepper. Scatter the garlic and rosemary around the pan, between the mushrooms. Pour about three-quarters of the bottle of beer over the mushrooms. Don't drink that last bit! Seriously, you will need it right at the end.

Pop the roasting pan into the oven for 10 to 12 minutes. Using tongs, flip the mushrooms over and gently give them a good push or two in the pan, so the gill sides are coated in the juicy beer-oil mixture. Flip the mushrooms back over and roast for another 10 minutes, or until the juices have reduced and caramelized.

Remove the roasting pan from the oven and arrange the mushrooms on serving plates. Set the roasting pan over medium heat. Remember that leftover beer? Good. Deglaze the pan with it: Get the beer bubbling for a minute or two while you use a wooden spoon to scrape up all the sticky goodness from the bottom of the pan. Once the beer has reduced a little, pour the pan juices over the mushrooms. Serve the mushrooms whole or sliced on the diagonal as you would a steak.

POLPETTE DI CECI (CHICKPEA BALLS)

I know what you're thinking, *Chickpea balls? Skip. Maybe for my pain-in-the-ass vegetarian cousin.* As you no doubt know by now, I love vegetables. There are quite a few vegetarian dishes on the menu at our restaurants, but I don't usually categorize them that way. They are just great dishes, made with fresh local produce, that happen to pass muster for those who don't eat meat. They are not a substitution for a meat dish, they would not be better with the inclusion of meat, and in terms of flavor and texture, there is zero compromise. They are delicious—full stop.

I also love how these little guys elevate a humble, inexpensive ingredient. When they are paired with a slightly bitter, slightly sweet escarole salad and a rustic pasta dressed with best-quality olive oil, garlic, and dried chile, you're set. They'd also be amazing served over a lightly dressed bed of arugula, with the residual heat wilting the greens.

Serves 2

½ cup dried chickpeas
2 bay leaves, preferably fresh
Fine sea salt
1 russet or very large Yukon Gold
   potato (about ¾ pound), peeled and
   cut into medium dice
Grated zest of 2 lemons
About ¼ cup chopped fresh flat-leaf
   parsley

1 garlic clove, chopped
4 large eggs, preferably free-range
1 tablespoon crushed red pepper
   flakes
2½ ounces Parmigiano-Reggiano,
   coarsely grated
Freshly ground black pepper
1 cup dried bread crumbs
Vegetable oil for shallow-frying

Put the chickpeas in a medium bowl, cover with cold water by 2 inches, and soak for 12 hours (either in the fridge or on the counter). Drain and rinse the chickpeas.

Put the chickpeas in a medium saucepan, add the bay leaves and 8 cups water, and bring to a boil over high heat. Reduce the heat to maintain a steady, active simmer and cook, uncovered, until the chickpeas are tender, 40 to 60 minutes (older beans will take longer to cook)—about halfway through the cooking time, add a generous teaspoon of salt to the simmering water. When the chickpeas are fully cooked, drain and set aside to cool.

Meanwhile, bring a small saucepan of salted water to a boil. Add the potato and cook until fork-tender, 15 to 20 minutes. Drain the potatoes and put through a food mill into a medium bowl.

When the chickpeas are completely cool, pulse half of them in a food processor until fairly smooth. Roughly mash the rest of the chickpeas with a fork in a large bowl—not too much; texture is key here. Add the pureed chickpeas, mashed potato, lemon zest, parsley, garlic, 1 of the eggs, the pepper flakes, and about three-quarters of the Parmigiano and, using a wooden spoon, mix well. Season with salt and black pepper to taste and mix again.

Moisten your hands so they're just damp and shape the chickpea mixture into balls the size of golf balls, setting them on a large plate as you

shape them. You should end up with about 18 balls.

Line a tray or large plate with parchment paper. Lightly beat the remaining 3 eggs in a medium shallow bowl. Put the bread crumbs in a small shallow bowl. Coat each ball in the egg, letting the excess drip off, then dredge in the bread crumbs and place on the lined tray.

Pour about ½ inch of oil into a large deep skillet and heat until hot. Working in batches, carefully add the balls to the hot oil, without crowding, and fry until golden brown and crisp, about 15 minutes on each side. Transfer to paper towels to drain and season the balls with salt and pepper while they're still hot.

Serve warm, finishing the balls with a sprinkling of the remaining Parmigiano.

CHICKEN CACCIATORE

My most cherished possession is the Silver Seal pot I inherited from my grandmother. That battered old cast-aluminum Dutch oven is also the only material object I have from her. It is my inheritance in a way, and it is the perfect one. In that pot, which she bought sometime in the 1930s, she cooked countless meals for her family, for her children and grandchildren. My favorite dish that came out of its magic depths? Chicken cacciatore. There was nothing better than walking into her house and smelling that aromatic braised chicken, the heady bay leaves, the bright tomatoes. No matter how cold it was, that scent warmed me all the way to my bones, and to this day it is a dish I associate with warmth and sustenance. We all have that kind of dish, the one that is a reference for home, that takes us back to family, that connects us to our past and our people. And so often that dish is chicken in a pot, be it the French coq au vin, Mexican chicken in a rich mole sauce, or this Italian chicken stew. And when you set the pot on the table and lift the lid, you'll release a cloud of fragrant steam that will fill your house—and your family's memory banks. This recipe is a valentine to my grandmother.

Note: If you feel hesitant about cutting up the whole chicken, when you're buying your bird, take the opportunity to bond with your butcher— ask where your chicken is from and request that he (or she) cut it up for you.

Serves 4

1 free-range chicken (about
   3 pounds)
¼ cup extra virgin olive oil
1 large white or yellow onion,
   quartered
5 garlic cloves, smashed and peeled
4 bay leaves, preferably fresh

1½ cups white wine
One 28-ounce can whole tomatoes
A pinch of crushed red pepper flakes
A pinch of dried oregano, preferably
   wild
Fine sea salt and freshly ground black
   pepper

Preheat the oven to 375°F.

Cut your chicken into 8 pieces: 2 breast halves, 2 wings, 2 thighs, and 2 drumsticks (you can save the neck and backbone for making stock).

Set a large Dutch oven over medium-high heat and add the olive oil. When the oil is hot, add the chicken, in batches, and sear the pieces until

In my grandmother's kitchen circa 1975 with Grandma Anna and Aunt Filomena. That very same silver seal pot on the stove remains one of my most prized possessions, and hopefully it will be for my kids as well.

golden brown all over, 2 to 3 minutes per side. Transfer to a plate and set aside.

Add the onion, garlic, and bay leaves to the pot, reduce the heat to medium, and cook for 3 to 4 minutes, stirring occasionally, to get the veggies coated in the drippings and charred bits. Return all the chicken to the pot and give it a gentle stir to help marry everything, then add the wine, increase the heat to medium-high, and let it bubble for about 5 minutes. When the wine has reduced by about half, add the tomatoes, with their juices, and use a wooden spoon to gently crush the tomatoes and bring everything together. Season with the red pepper flakes, oregano, salt, and pepper.

Cover the pot with a tight-fitting lid and pop it into the oven for 1 hour. Then uncover, increase the oven temperature to 400°F, and bake, uncovered, for 20 to 30 minutes, until the meat slips easily off the bone. Serve hot.

BRACIOLE

My great-aunt Margie was the best cook in the family. We lived with
her in the Bronx when I was a little kid. This was one of her specialties.
Making braciole was all about the art of stretching a protein—in one sense,
literally—to feed as many people as possible. You take a cheap cut of meat
and beat it—literally—into something yielding. Then you stuff it with bread
crumbs and herbs so it's even more substantial and braise it in sauce until
it's meltingly tender. One of the great miracles of braciole is that it can only
get better as it is transformed by the slow heat; 5 or 10 minutes longer isn't
going to make or break it. It is a dish that comes out of real kitchens, where
people are by necessity getting on with life while still making something
special. Like meatballs or *polpettone*, braciole is a deeply homey food that is
tweaked from family to family—there are probably as many variations on it
as there are Italian and Italian American families. I hope you enjoy this one
as much as I do.

Serves 6

FOR THE STUFFING
½ cup whole milk
A handful of fine dried bread crumbs
A handful of chopped fresh flat-leaf
  parsley

1 ounce Parmigiano-Reggiano,
  coarsely grated
¼ cup raisins
2 garlic cloves, finely chopped

FOR THE BRACIOLE
One 2-pound rump roast, cut into
  12 slices (ask the butcher to slice the
  meat for you)

Fine sea salt and freshly ground black
  pepper

FOR THE SAUCE
3 tablespoons extra virgin olive oil, or
  as needed
2 tablespoons unsalted butter, or as
  needed
2 small white or yellow onions,
  chopped
2 garlic cloves, finely chopped

3 bay leaves, preferably fresh
½ cup red wine
¾ cup Crushed Tomato Sauce (page 8)
6 cups chicken stock
Fine sea salt
A good pinch of crushed red pepper
  flakes

To make the stuffing: Combine the milk and bread crumbs in a medium bowl and let soak for about 10 minutes.

Drain the bread in a fine-mesh sieve (discard the milk) and squeeze out any remaining milk with your hands. Return the bread to the bowl, add the parsley, Parmigiano, raisins, and garlic and give everything a good stir.

To make the braciole: Using a meat tenderizer, gently pound each slice of beef as thin as you can get it, starting with the fine-toothed side of the mallet and then switching to a smooth side to finish flattening it to about ⅛ inch thick. Set a slice on the work surface with a short end facing you and season with salt and pepper. Spread 2 tablespoons of the stuffing along the edge of the meat closest to you, leaving a ½-inch border, then fold the sides of the meat over the edges of the stuffing. Roll up into a compact roll and secure the end flap with a toothpick and transfer to a plate. Repeat with the remaining beef slices and stuffing. Season the outside of the rolls with salt and pepper.

To make the sauce: Set a large Dutch oven over medium heat. Add the olive oil and butter and heat until hot. Add as many braciole as will fit in a single layer, making sure not to overcrowd the pot (cook in batches if necessary, adding more oil and butter as needed) and cook, turning occasionally, until golden on all sides, about 7 minutes. Transfer the braciole to a plate and set aside.

Add the onions and garlic to the pot and sauté until the onions are translucent, 5 to 7 minutes. Add the bay leaves and return the beef to the pot. Add the wine, increase the heat to medium-high, bring the wine to a boil, and cook until it has reduced by half.

Add the tomato sauce and stock, season with salt and the red pepper flakes, and bring to a boil. Reduce the heat to a simmer and cook, partially covered, for 2 to 2½ hours. To check if the beef is ready, use two forks to gently pull at the meat in opposite directions—it should pull apart easily. Remove the pot from the heat, transfer the braciole to a plate, and let sit for a few minutes, just until they have cooled enough that you can pull the toothpicks out.

Arrange 2 braciole on each plate, spoon some of the sauce over them, and serve.

SLOW-ROASTED LAMB NECK

Lamb necks are great and super flavorful, with enough fat and bones to make this dish rich and silky. They taste a lot like veal shanks, the cut of meat you're more likely to see in a preparation like this. In fact, at our restaurants we did first set out to do an iconic Milanese osso buco, but we have great lamb here in Arizona, so using it made sense. If you reinterpret a classic dish, you have the opportunity to explore new dimensions—and to connect with your audience in unexpected ways. In eating lamb necks, you really connect with the animal. "Lesser" cuts allow you to give the animal your gratitude and impart a measure of dignity to its sacrifice. We serve this dish simply, with chickpeas and a tangle of beautiful dark greens.

Serves 4

4 bone-in lamb neck slices (6 to 8 ounces each)
Fine sea salt and freshly ground black pepper
¼ cup extra virgin olive oil
2 large carrots, peeled and chopped into ½-inch pieces
2 celery stalks, chopped into ½-inch pieces

2 white or yellow onions, chopped into ½-inch pieces
3 garlic cloves, smashed and peeled
¼ cup Crushed Tomato Sauce (page 8)
1 cup red wine
3 quarts lamb or chicken stock
12 bay leaves, preferably fresh

Preheat the oven to 275°F.

Season the lamb liberally with salt and pepper. Heat the olive oil in a large Dutch oven over medium-high heat. When the oil is hot but not smoking, add the lamb necks and sear, turning occasionally, until nicely browned all over, about 7 minutes per side. Transfer the lamb to a plate.

Add the carrots, celery, onions, and garlic to the pot, reduce the heat to medium, and cook, stirring the vegetables occasionally with a wooden spoon, until you get some good color on them; use the wooden spoon as you go to scrape all the crusty lamb drippings from the bottom of the pot as the vegetables caramelize. Add the tomato sauce, stir to coat the vegetables with the sauce, and cook for about 5 minutes.

Deglaze the pot with the wine, scraping up the browned bits with the wooden spoon, and let the wine bubble gently until it reduces by about half. Add the stock and bay leaves and season with salt and pepper. Return the lamb to the pot, increase the heat to high, and bring the stock to a boil, then remove the pot from the heat. Skim the surface of the stock of any fat or scum that has risen to the top.

Put the pot in the oven and cook the lamb necks for about 2 hours, turning them every half hour or so (you don't want them to stick and burn), until the meat is almost falling off the bone. Carefully remove the lamb from the pot and set aside.

Pour the braising liquid, with all the vegetables, into a blender or food processor (work in batches if necessary) and blitz until the vegetables are pureed.

Place a couple of tablespoons of the sauce in the bottom of each serving bowl, top with a slice of lamb neck, and drizzle with more sauce.

SOMETHING SWEET

EXTENDED TABLE

I've never really been a big dessert eater. A piece of fruit, some cheese, a bite of dark chocolate while I finish my glass of wine, a cold slice of watermelon with lime and salt on a hot day—these are my kind of treats: simple, focused, unfussy.

Dessert was not a big thing in our household when I was growing up, though my mom, Francesca, is a pretty amazing pastry cook. In fact, every Tuesday she prepares a special dessert at our pizzeria in Phoenix. We have customers who come in just for a slice of whatever she makes that day. But at home, we didn't end every dinner with dessert; instead, sweetness punctuated our days in a different way. It might be a beautiful brioche to enjoy with coffee; or a cannoli, oozing ricotta, studded with fruit and nuts, as an afternoon treat; or shards of icy granita cooling you from the inside out on a sweaty New York City summer day. Occasionally it would be a small, comforting bowl of pudding or custard at the end of the evening meal, a little something sweet to close the day.

But I like the idea of dessert as an extension of the meal. Dessert gives us the opportunity to linger at the table. It gives us pleasure. Usually by the time we reach dessert, we're no longer hungry—so it is not something we eat because we need to. And for that reason, there is something inherently celebratory about dessert. It's about taking the time to enjoy a little bit of life's sweetness.

Years ago, I went to stay with a great-uncle in Friuli. Every night after dinner, he would reach up into a cupboard and bring down a bar of chocolate. He would ceremoniously, almost reverentially, unwrap it and carefully break off one square for each of us. To watch him was almost a religious experience. Then

he'd wrap the bar back up, just as carefully, and put it away before enjoying his one beautiful, glossy square. One square was more than enough of that perfect thing.

Sometimes you just need to get out of the way of such perfection. When cherries are in season, why mess around? Wash them, put them in a beautiful bowl, and serve. That's why I've chosen not to call this chapter "Dessert." What you'll find here is a series of opportunities: to linger at a table, by yourself or in the company of those you love, over a little something sweet and a cup of coffee or a last glass of wine; to celebrate the moment of truly ripe fruit or a delicious homemade cake, and the fact that you have the opportunity to celebrate; or just to punctuate your day with a moment of sweetness.

RHUBARB RICOTTA PUDDING (BY WAY OF CANNOLI)

I love cannoli. I love the crisp crunch of the fried dough giving way to the soft, rich filling—creamy ricotta studded with fruit or chocolate or crushed cookies, or flecked with spices, sweetened with sugar or honey. Cannoli are one of Sicily's greatest gifts to the world. Perhaps there should be a specific time of day dedicated to eating them. The English have tea— why shouldn't we have some quiet time when we can contemplate our souls with a cannoli and a cup of coffee (or a fragrant tea)? This dessert is my homage to that beloved pastry. The richness of the creamy filling is offset by the tart, tangy rhubarb. I like to use lemon cookies here, but shortbread would be great, too, as would chocolate chip cookies. Or any cookie you love.

Serves 4

1¼ cups granulated sugar

Grated zest of 1 lemon

½ cup water

2 medium rhubarb stalks, trimmed and cut into 1-inch pieces

1 vanilla bean

1 cup fresh ricotta, drained (see box)

1½ tablespoons fresh lemon juice

¼ cup powdered sugar

¼ teaspoon ground cinnamon

¼ teaspoon freshly grated nutmeg

4 small cookies, such as Lemon Cookies (page 190), roughly chopped (about ½ cup)

About ½ ounce dark chocolate, finely grated (optional)

Combine the granulated sugar, lemon zest, and water in a medium saucepan and bring to a boil over medium-high heat, stirring to dissolve the sugar. Add the rhubarb and cook until soft to the touch, about 2 minutes; you want the fruit to still be a little firm. Remove from the heat and set aside to cool. (As it cools, the rhubarb will cook a little more.) Cover and refrigerate until needed.

Split the vanilla bean in half and scrape the seeds into a medium bowl. (Discard the pod, or reserve it for another use, such as vanilla sugar.)

DRAINING RICOTTA

When making cannoli, you want to drain your ricotta, or you risk soggy cannoli shells. The same holds true here—you want the cookie crumbles in the filling to keep their texture. To drain ricotta quickly, place a large piece of cheesecloth in a bowl. Scoop the ricotta onto the cheesecloth, gather up the edges of the cloth so you have a bundle of ricotta, twist them together, and squeeze as much water out of the ricotta as possible.

Add the ricotta, lemon juice, powdered sugar, cinnamon, and nutmeg and, using a whisk or hand mixer, beat until the ingredients are well blended and smooth. Gently fold in the cookies and the chocolate (if using). Don't overmix, or the filling will become muddled.

Scoop some of the rhubarb into the bottom of each of four mason jars or glasses, followed by some of the filling, then repeat. Finish up with the remaining rhubarb on top. Serve.

MAMA'S SIMPLE CUSTARD

This is a type of crème caramel, if you like—my mother's silky-smooth version, with deep vanilla flavor. The custard should be served in one bowl at the table—let each person slide a spoon in and serve themselves. Make this the day before you want to serve it, if you can, so it has time to chill and set.

Serves 8

Special Equipment:
Pastry brush; 9-inch deep-dish glass pie plate

FOR THE CARAMEL
1 cup sugar
2 tablespoons water

FOR THE CUSTARD
8 large eggs, preferably free-range
½ cup superfine sugar

4 cups light cream or half-and-half
2 teaspoons pure vanilla extract

Preheat the oven to 350°F.

To make the caramel: Set the pie plate next to the stove. Put the sugar and water in a small saucepan and stir constantly over medium heat until the sugar dissolves. Wet the pastry brush with water. Then cook the sugar mixture without stirring, brushing down the sides of the pan with the brush as necessary to remove any sugar crystals, until the caramel is a beautiful golden color; immediately pour it into the bottom of the pie plate.

Bring a kettle of water to a boil.

Meanwhile, to make the custard: In a large bowl, beat the eggs with a hand mixer on high speed until slightly thickened and foamy, about 3 minutes. Beat in the sugar. Add the cream and vanilla and beat until foamy. Pour into the pie plate.

Set the pie plate in a roasting pan large enough to hold it comfortably. Pour enough boiling water into the roasting pan to come about halfway up the sides of the pie plate. Place the roasting pan in the oven and bake for

50 to 55 minutes, until the custard is just set; the top will be lightly browned. A knife inserted in the center should come out clean. Remove the roasting pan and let the custard cool completely in the water, about 1 hour. (Cooling it in the water bath will prevent cracks.)

Remove the pie plate from the water bath and refrigerate the custard until chilled, at least 6 hours or, preferably, overnight. To unmold, run a paring knife around the edges of the custard to release it. Invert a large platter (with a lip, to contain the caramel sauce) over the custard and carefully invert both the platter and pie plate, shaking the pie plate a few times to release the custard, then lift off the pie plate. (If the custard doesn't release, set the pie plate in a roasting pan filled with ½ inch of very hot water, then repeat the process.) Spoon any caramel remaining in the pie plate over the custard and serve.

CAROLINA RICE PUDDING

Here is an example of falling in love with an ingredient and its journey and then finding a place for it to elevate something comforting and familiar. This pudding is delicious with some whipped cream or a spoon of jam.

When my good friend Glenn Roberts from Anson Mills shared with me the amazing history of Carolina Gold rice and all of the hard work they put into making sure that it did not disappear from our culinary landscape, I wanted to ensure that we found a place for it on our menu. This was a commitment that would help illuminate not only how delicious it was but how we, along with our farmers, have a responsibility and an opportunity to know who we are through our culinary history.

Serves 6 to 8

1 quart whole milk
2 cups heavy cream
1 vanilla bean
½ cup Carolina Gold or Arborio or other
   short-grain rice
1½ cups sugar
1 teaspoon fine sea salt

Combine the milk and cream in a large heavy saucepan. Split the vanilla bean, scrape out the seeds, and add to the milk-cream mixture; add the scraped pod as well. Bring the liquid to a boil over medium heat, stirring to prevent the mixture from scorching. Add the rice, sugar, and salt and give it a good stir, then reduce the heat to a simmer and cook for 1½ hours, stirring every 10 minutes or so to prevent the rice from sticking to the bottom of the pan and burning.

Remove from the heat and let the pudding cool a little—it will thicken as it sits. Serve warm or cold.

LEMON COOKIES

At our restaurants, we serve these sweet-tart cookies on a little plate alongside coffee or tea. They're a perfect note on which to end a meal. Again, this is about seizing the opportunity of optimal ingredients. When lemons are at their best in the winter and spring months, make these. You can substitute a little clementine or orange juice if you want—any citrus, really.

Makes 2 dozen cookies

½ pound (2 sticks) unsalted butter,
   at room temperature
¾ cup powdered sugar
1½ cups all-purpose flour
1 teaspoon grated lemon zest
1½ teaspoons fresh lemon juice
½ teaspoon vanilla bean paste or
   pure vanilla extract

FOR THE LEMON GLAZE
1½ cups powdered sugar
2 tablespoons fresh lemon juice
½ teaspoon vanilla bean paste or
   pure vanilla extract

1 teaspoon grated lemon zest, for garnish

VANILLA

Vanilla extract is made through, well, extraction—vanilla beans are macerated in water and alcohol for several months and then the fragrant liquid is strained. Vanilla bean paste is basically vanilla seeds in a sweet vanilla syrup. Though it's more expensive than vanilla extract, the flavor is huge, and I love how it flecks your food with the tiny seeds. You can use it 1:1 in any recipe that calls for vanilla extract. Vanilla bean paste is available at gourmet markets and online.

Preheat the oven to 350°F. Line a large baking sheet with parchment paper.

Combine the butter and powdered sugar in a large bowl and beat with a hand mixer on medium speed until light and fluffy. With the mixer on low speed, gradually add the flour, beating until incorporated. Add the lemon zest, lemon juice, and vanilla, mixing until combined.

Scoop up a level tablespoon of dough, roll it into a small log about 2½ inches long and ½ inch in diameter, and place on the baking sheet. Repeat with the remaining dough, spacing the logs 2 inches apart.

Bake for 15 to 17 minutes, until the edges of the cookies just begin to brown. Remove from the oven and cool completely on the pan on a rack. (The cookies are very fragile when just out of the oven.)

To make the lemon glaze: Combine the powdered sugar, lemon juice, and vanilla in a bowl and whisk together to make a smooth glaze.

Transfer the cookies to a clean sheet of parchment paper. Drizzle with the lemon glaze and sprinkle with the lemon zest. Let the glaze set before serving.

FARRO BISCOTTI
WITH MANDARIN, ALMOND, AND ANISE

Biscotti are the perfect lesson in what I like to call "appropriating the vehicle." By that, I mean you take a dry, raspy cookie and activate it, or bring it to life, by dunking it in coffee or a good Vin Santo. Nowadays I think of biscotti as the trusty workhorse of the cookie world: solid, dependable, always at the ready.

If you like, use almonds with their skins still on, which will add another textural dimension to the cookie. And if you like soft cookies like me: After the first bake, save a few sliced biscotti to eat while they're still warm, then put the rest back in the oven for the second bake.

Makes 28 biscotti

1 teaspoon aniseeds
1½ cups all-purpose flour
1 cup fine cornmeal or polenta
1½ teaspoons baking powder
¼ teaspoon fine sea salt
9 tablespoons unsalted butter, at room
   temperature

1½ cups sugar
2 large eggs, preferably free-range
1 teaspoon anise extract
Grated zest of 1 mandarin orange
1 cup blanched whole almonds

Position a rack in the center of the oven and preheat the oven to 350°F. Line a large baking sheet with parchment paper.

Toast the aniseeds in a small dry skillet just until fragrant. Transfer to a small plate and set aside.

Whisk together the flour, cornmeal, baking powder, and salt in a bowl.

Combine the butter and sugar in a large bowl and beat with a hand mixer until smooth and creamy. Add the eggs one at a time, beating well after each addition. Add the anise extract, toasted aniseeds, orange zest, and almonds and mix well. Add the flour mixture and beat just until incorporated.

Divide the dough in half. Put one portion of dough next to one long side of the prepared baking sheet and shape into a 12 x 4-inch loaf. Repeat with the second portion of dough, leaving ample space between the logs (they will spread during baking). Bake for 15 minutes, or until the dough starts to crack on top. Remove from the oven and set aside to cool for 15 to 20 minutes. (Leave the oven on.)

Using a serrated knife, slice each log crosswise into 14 biscotti. Lay them out cut side down on the lined baking sheet and bake for 5 minutes. Flip the biscotti and bake for another 5 minutes, or until a beautiful golden color on both sides. Transfer the biscotti to a wire rack and cool completely. Store in an airtight container.

APPLE CAKE

There always seemed to be a cake at hand in our house when I was growing up—often this apple cake. It was handed down from my maternal grandfather's side of the family, who hailed from Carrara, Tuscany. I remember sitting down with my mom, not having to say anything, just enjoying the cake and the silence together. The cake is also good with some lightly whipped cream, or maybe a slice of great cheddar or Gruyère. The only thing that could possibly make it any better would be to have it with a steaming mug of apple cider or some spiced mulled wine. Happy days.

Makes one 9 x 13-inch cake

⅔ cup raisins
½ cup dark rum
1½ pounds tart green apples (2 large), such as Granny Smith, peeled, cored, and cut into ½-inch pieces (about 5 cups)
2 cups packed light brown sugar
3 cups all-purpose flour
2 teaspoons baking powder
1 teaspoon freshly grated nutmeg
1 teaspoon ground allspice
½ teaspoon fine sea salt

2 large eggs, preferably free-range, lightly beaten
1 cup high-quality extra virgin olive oil or vegetable oil
¼ cup orange or apple juice
2 teaspoons pure vanilla extract
1 tablespoon chopped crystallized ginger
1 cup walnuts, lightly toasted and chopped
1 cup dried cranberries

Position a rack in the center of the oven and preheat the oven to 350°F. Lightly grease 9 x 13-inch baking pan and dust with flour.

Combine the raisins with the rum in a small bowl and let them soak while you prepare the rest of the ingredients.

Combine the apples and brown sugar in a large bowl and stir to mix. Let stand for 15 minutes.

Whisk together the flour, baking powder, nutmeg, allspice, and salt in a medium bowl.

Add the eggs, olive oil, and juice to the apples and stir well. Add the flour mixture, vanilla, ginger, walnuts, and cranberries and mix well. Add the raisins, with their liquid, and mix well.

Pour or spoon the batter into the greased cake pan and bake for 55 to 60 minutes, until the cake is golden on top and fragrant. To check for doneness, insert a toothpick or thin skewer into the middle of it—it should come out clean. Let the cake cool for 30 minutes in the pan on a wire rack.

Turn the cake out onto a platter or serve directly from the pan, warm or at room temperature. The cake will keep, covered, for up to 1 week.

SEASONAL FRUIT CROSTATA

Crostata is a classic Italian dessert; simple and rustic, it's a free-form fruit tart that doesn't benefit from attempts to overkill. The crisp, sweet pastry that is its foundation is the perfect foil for whatever height-of-the-season inspiration looks irresistible at your local farmers' market (or orchard) that day.

Serves 6 to 8

3 cups sliced seasonal fruit (peaches, plums, figs, and apricots are all terrific) or halved cherries
¾ cup granulated sugar
1 tablespoon cornstarch
Grated zest of 1 lemon

1 tablespoon fresh lemon juice
1 teaspoon ground cinnamon
Basic Tart Dough (recipe follows)
1½ tablespoons heavy cream
Powdered sugar, for dusting

Preheat the oven to 350°F. Line a baking sheet with parchment paper.

Combine the fruit, granulated sugar, cornstarch, lemon zest, lemon juice, and cinnamon in a large bowl and mix well.

On a lightly floured surface, roll the dough out into a thin circle roughly 11 inches in diameter. Transfer the dough to the baking sheet. Spoon the fruit onto the dough, leaving a ¾-inch border all around. Fold the edges of the dough over the fruit, pleating the dough as necessary. Brush the edges of the dough with the cream.

Bake the crostata for 50 to 55 minutes, until the crust is golden brown. Let cool for 20 minutes, then dust with powdered sugar and serve warm. Or let cool to room temperature and dust with powdered sugar before serving.

BASIC TART DOUGH

Makes enough for 1 crostata

1½ cups all-purpose flour
½ teaspoon fine sea salt
10 tablespoons (1¼ sticks) unsalted
  butter, at room temperature

1 tablespoon powdered sugar
2 large egg yolks, preferably free-
  range

Combine the flour, salt, butter, and powdered sugar in a large bowl and beat with a hand mixer on medium speed until the mixture resembles coarse crumbs. (You can also use a stand mixer fitted with the paddle attachment or a food processor.) Add the egg yolks and mix until they are incorporated and the dough just begins to come together.

Turn out the dough and shape it into a disk. Wrap in plastic wrap and let rest in the fridge for at least 1 hour. The dough can be refrigerated for up to 1 week. One hour before using, remove it from the fridge and let it come to room temperature.

MY FAVORITE SPONGE CAKE

This cake, a favorite in our house when I was growing up, came from my grandma Daisy—my mom's mom—who had had the recipe at least since the turn of the last century. My mom, Francesca, says the first time she ever made it was in the late 1950s, and thereafter it became her go-to dessert, especially if we had company for dinner. With its high egg content, it has a texture similar to that of a génoise, an Italian sponge cake (a staple in French baking) that gets its volume from the air beaten into the eggs. It is a terrific base for fillings such as jam, custard, or whipped cream and fresh fruit. My mom would often slice it horizontally into two layers and then fill it. I like to brush the bottom layer with rum, wait a moment or two, and spread it with some of the ricotta mixture from the Rhubarb Ricotta Pudding (page 184, with a little extra grated orange zest added to it). Then I brush a little more rum on the cut side of the top layer, flip it carefully so the rum side faces down, and top the whole thing with whipped cream. It's even better when it sits overnight in the fridge so all the flavors have a chance to marry.

Francesca's tip: The 10-minute beating time is from the original recipe, so go with it. Over one hundred years of cooking can't be so wrong! You can replace the vanilla extract with almond extract or lemon zest. If you use lemon zest, a lemon curd filling, optimally homemade in season, would be amazing.

Note that you will need a 3-inch-deep 9 x 13-inch baking pan for this cake; these are available online and at specialty housewares shops.

Makes one 9 x 13-inch cake

Special Equipment:
A 9 x 13-inch baking pan that is 3 inches deep

2 cups all-purpose flour
2 teaspoons baking powder
¼ teaspoon fine sea salt
10 large eggs, preferably free-range

2 cups sugar
1 teaspoon pure vanilla extract
1 teaspoon fresh lemon juice

Preheat the oven to 350°F. Grease the 9 x 13 x 3-inch baking pan. Line it with parchment paper, then grease and lightly flour the parchment paper.

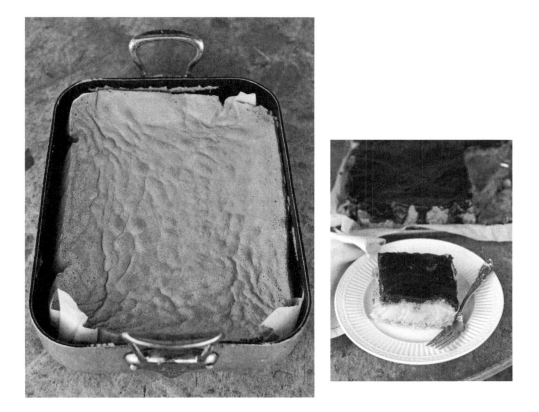

Sift the flour, baking powder, and salt into a bowl and whisk to mix thoroughly.

Crack the eggs into the bowl of a stand mixer fitted with the whisk attachment (or use a large bowl and a hand mixer). Beat on medium speed just to combine the whites and yolks. Slowly beat in the sugar, then increase the speed to high and beat for 10 minutes. (This is really important—it will give the cake the proper structure by introducing air.) Beat in the vanilla and lemon juice. Mixing on low speed, gradually add the flour mixture, mixing just until incorporated.

Scrape the batter into the baking pan. Bake for 55 to 60 minutes, until the cake is golden and a toothpick or a skewer inserted into the middle of the cake comes out clean. Let the cake cool for 20 minutes in its pan on a rack. The cake will deflate slightly as it cools; don't sweat it.

Run a paring knife around the edges of the pan to release the cake and invert it onto a tray or a platter. Carefully lift away the parchment paper and discard. The cake will keep, wrapped, for 2 to 3 days.

THREE ITALIAN ICES

When I was growing up in New York, the passage of the seasons from spring to summer was marked every year by one unmistakable sign: all the Italian bakeries wheeling out their little ice cream carts or freezer cabinets. There was always chocolate ice, always lemon ice, and sometimes a creamy hazelnut one. I couldn't have loved it more—the lure of the ices and long summer days ahead. There was something magical about the ritual of walking out together as a family after dinner, when the night was still and warm, and getting that paper cup of ice. You always ate it right there, on the sidewalk out in front of the shop, or on the walk home. The paper cup was as important an ingredient as the taste of the ice itself, and for that reason we often serve ices that way at our restaurants. I love to see people twisting the cup and squeezing the last three or four spoonfuls out of the bottom of it, conjuring up their own memories with each mouthful of icy delight.

Although you may think of ices as the more familiar pure fruit ices, some Italian ices are actually milk-based—leaning toward sherbet. The Lemon Ice here is a straightforward fruit ice, but the Chocolate and Nutmeg Ices are both made with milk.

CHOCOLATE ICE

Makes about 1 quart

Special Equipment:
Ice cream maker

5 ounces good-quality bittersweet chocolate (80% to 85% cacao), finely chopped
1 quart whole milk
1 cup sugar
2 vanilla beans or 2 teaspoons vanilla paste or pure vanilla extract

Place the chocolate in a heatproof medium bowl.

Combine the milk and sugar in a large saucepan. Split the vanilla beans and scrape the seeds into the milk mixture. Set the saucepan over medium heat and bring the mixture to a boil, stirring to prevent the milk from scorching. As soon as the milk boils, pour it over the chocolate. Let sit for 2 minutes, so the chocolate melts, then stir with a wooden spoon to mix well.

Set up a large ice bath (a bowl filled with equal amounts of ice and water). Set the bowl of chocolate mixture in the ice bath and stir occasionally until the mixture is cool, about 20 minutes. Then cover and refrigerate until well chilled, at least 4 hours.

Churn the chocolate mixture in the ice cream maker according to the manufacturer's instructions. Transfer to an airtight container and freeze until firm, at least 1 hour.

Serve the ice in paper cups or small bowls.

NUTMEG ICE

Makes about 1 quart

Special Equipment:
Ice cream maker

1 quart whole milk
¾ cup sugar
1½ teaspoons freshly grated nutmeg
½ cinnamon stick

Set up a large ice bath (a bowl filled with equal amounts of ice and water).

Combine the milk, sugar, nutmeg, and cinnamon stick in a large saucepan and bring to a boil over medium heat, stirring to prevent the milk from scorching. Immediately remove the saucepan from the heat and pour the mixture into a bowl. Set the bowl in the ice bath and stir occasionally until the mixture is cool, about 20 minutes. Then cover and refrigerate until well chilled, at least 4 hours. Remove the cinnamon stick.

Churn the mixture in the ice cream maker according to the manufacturer's instructions; it will still be somewhat slushy. Transfer to an airtight container and freeze until firm, at least 1 hour.

Serve the ice in paper cups or small bowls.

LEMON ICE

Makes about 1 quart

Special Equipment:
Ice cream maker

¾ cup sugar
2 tablespoons grated lemon zest
4 cups water
1 teaspoon Cointreau or Grand
    Marnier
1⅓ cups fresh lemon juice (8 or
    9 lemons)

Combine the sugar, lemon zest, and water in a medium saucepan and bring to a boil over medium heat, stirring to dissolve the sugar. Remove the mixture from the heat, pour into a large bowl, and allow to cool completely. Add the Cointreau or Grand Marnier and lemon juice and stir to mix thoroughly. Cover and refrigerate until well chilled, at least 4 hours.

Churn the mixture in the ice cream maker according to the manufacturer's instructions. Transfer to an airtight container and freeze until firm, at least 1 hour.

Serve the ice in paper cups or small bowls.

ACKNOWLEDGMENTS

Acknowledgments for this book could fill a whole other book, just with gratitude, but here goes a few:

To my publisher, Dan Halpern, for asking and believing, and my agent, Felicity Blunt, who gave much more than I could have expected in guiding me through the publishing process.

To the writers—all of them, including Gary Nabhan and Judith Sutton—and my editor, Gabriella Doob, and all the crew at Ecco. What a nightmare dealing with my mumbling and mind chatter; I had no idea finding my voice would take such a village. The only thing I knew going in was that pictures are always the most powerful part of a book's inspiration. My dear friend photographer David Loftus—well, I will let his work speak for itself.

Then there is my team: Robbie "the rock" Tutlewski, who is a true gift and talent; my brother, Marco, for his support and dedication; and each and every hand and heart in my kitchens—past and present. My pal Jimmy for, well, too much to list and Seth Sulka whose help in this book (from finding the right publisher to getting it to the shelf) and my life is immeasurable.

To my mother, Francesca, for letting me lick the spoon and my father, Leo, for making art omnipresent. And to my beautiful wife, Mia, and our children, Nina, Leo, and the baby to be named later, I dedicate every beat of my heart.